WUTHERING HEIGHTS

The Writing in the Margin

TWAYNE'S MASTERWORK STUDIES

Robert Lecker, General Editor

WUTHERING HEIGHTS

The Writing in the Margin

Maggie Berg

TWAYNE PUBLISHERS
An Imprint of Simon & Schuster Macmillan
New York

PRENTICE HALL INTERNATIONAL
London Mexico City New Delhi Singapore Sydney Toronto

Twayne's Masterwork Studies No. 163

Wuthering Heights: The Writing in the Margin
Maggie Berg

Twayne Publishers
An Imprint of Simon & Schuster Macmillan
1633 Broadway
New York, New York 10019

Library of Congress Cataloging-in-Publication Data

Berg, Maggie.
    Wuthering Heights / Maggie Berg.
       p. cm. — (Masterworks studies ; 163)
    Includes bibliographical references and index.
    ISBN 0-8057-8051-3 (cloth). — ISBN 0-8057-8101-3 (cloth)
    1. Brontë, Emily, 1818–1848. Wuthering Heights. 2. Literature
and society—England—Yorkshire—History—19th century. 3. Women
and literature—England—Yorkshire—History—19th century.
4. Inheritance and succession in literature. 5. Yorkshire
(England)—In literature. 6. Sex (Psychology) in literature.
7. Family violence in literature. 8. Patriarchy in literature.
I. Title. II. Series: Twayne's masterwork studies : no. 163.
PR4172.W73B47   1996
823'.8—dc20   96–31198
                                              CIP

10 9 8 7 6 5 4 3 2   (hc)
10 9 8 7 6 5 4 3 2 1 (pb)

Printed in the United States of America

This book is dedicated to my sister Genevieve who first recommended Wuthering Heights *to me; also to my sisters Sarah and Rebecca, and my brother Giles.*

Contents

Emily Brontë
Courtesy of the National Portrait Gallery, London

Acknowledgments

I wish to thank Robert Lecker for his encouragement and his perceptive, judicious editing; Barbara Seeber and Scott Wallis for their help-
ful comments and proofreading; Julian Elce for his help with proofreading; Felix Brown for his invaluable assistance with computer
problems. Above all, I wish to thank Scott Wallis for his love and sup-
port and Rebecca Barrett-Wallis for the joy she gives me.

Chronology: Emily Brontë's Life and Works

1812	29 December, the Reverend Patrick Brontë marries Maria Branwell.
1814	April, Maria born.
1815	February, Elizabeth born. May, family moves to St. James's Church, Thornton.
1816	21 April, Charlotte born.
1817	26 June, Patrick Branwell born.
1818	30 July, Emily Jane born (fifth of six children). Maria (Emily's mother) ill.
1820	17 January, Anne born. The Brontës move to Haworth, Yorkshire.
1821	January, Elizabeth Branwell comes to care for her sick sister. 15 September, Maria dies, probably of cancer. Aunt Branwell remains to take care of the children.
1824	July, Maria and Elizabeth sent to Cowan Bridge School. August, Charlotte joins her sisters. November, Emily also there (age six).
1825	February, Maria sent home very ill; dies May. Elizabeth also very ill; dies June. Charlotte and Emily taken away from school.
1826	Charlotte (age ten), Branwell (age nine), Emily (age eight), and Anne (age six) begin "great plays" with Branwell's toy soldiers, which they chronicle at length in various forms.
1827	Emily and Charlotte collaborate on "secret plays" in shared bedroom.
1831	Charlotte goes to Roe Head School. Emily and Anne begin Gondal Chronicles.

1835	July, Emily goes to Roe Head School as pupil; Charlotte begins there as teacher. Emily very ill, sent home in October. Anne replaces her. Emily recovers quickly at home in Haworth.
1836	July 12, first extant poem by Emily: "Will the day be bright."
1837	September, Emily goes to teach at Law Hill School near Halifax; stays for about six months. Twenty extant poems by Emily.
1838	December, Emily at home again; 20 more poems.
1838–42	Over half of Emily's surviving poems written.
1842	February, Emily and Charlotte go to Pensionnat Heger in Brussels in order to educate themselves sufficiently to open own school. November, called home due to Aunt Branwell's illness; she dies before Emily and Charlotte arrive.
1843	Emily very happy and creative, alone at Haworth with her father.
1844	Emily begins to enter poems into two books—"Gondal Poems" and "E. J. B."
1845	All Brontës at home. School plan discarded by sisters. Charlotte discovers Emily's poems in lap desk. Although Emily is angry, Charlotte persuades her to try to publish a collection of poetry of all three sisters. December, *Wuthering Heights* begun.
1846	Sisters pay Aylott and Jones £40 for cost of publication of *Poems: by Currer, Ellis and Acton Bell,* which appears in May. Publishers not interested in three novels in progress—*Jane Eyre, Wuthering Heights,* and *Agnes Grey. Poems* receives little critical attention.
1847	July, T. C. Newby accepts *Wuthering Heights* and *Agnes Grey* for publication, but rejects Charlotte's *The Professor.* Smith, Elder & Co. willing to publish *Jane Eyre.* October, *Jane Eyre* published. December, *Wuthering Heights* and *Agnes Grey* published.
1848	Smith, Elder informs the "Bells" that novels are being offered to American publishers as work of single author. Charlotte and Anne go to London to prove their separate identities; becomes known for first time that Currer, Ellis, and Acton Bell are women. November, Emily very ill but refuses medical aid and struggles to maintain a normal routine. Anne also ill (dies September 1849). 19 December, Emily Brontë dies, immediately after agreeing to see a doctor. Newby had just announced

another forthcoming novel, which later leads to speculation that Charlotte destroyed manuscript of Emily's second novel.

1850   Charlotte publishes second edition of *Wuthering Heights* with textual emendations, "Editor's Preface" and "Biographical Notice."

LITERARY AND HISTORICAL CONTEXT

1

The Historical Context

It is difficult to place Emily Brontë in a historical and literary context: although we know a great deal about events and ideas during her short lifetime (1818–48), we know almost nothing about how she responded to them. No first-hand account exists of her life except for her sister Charlotte's brief and contradictory Preface and Biographical Notice to the second edition of *Wuthering Heights* and Elizabeth Gaskell's fleeting references in her *Life of Charlotte Brontë*.[1] As far as we know, Emily Brontë made no friends, and so wrote few letters (three survive); there are only two diary-fragments and two "Birthday Papers," all written with her sister Anne.[2] Charlotte emphasizes her sister's reclusiveness (38), and the latest Brontë biographer, Juliet Barker, repeats that the outside world made almost no impact on her.[3] Lyn Pykett rightly observes that Emily is "a figure glimpsed in the margins of her sister's life"(*LP*, 2). Emily Brontë clearly chose to be marginal: she was extremely reluctant to publish her poetry, was outraged when Charlotte found and read her manuscript without permission, and was unwilling to reveal her identity behind the pseudonym Ellis Bell (*JB*, 563).

Because we have so little direct evidence of Brontë's views—her poems are mainly dramatic, intended for an epic about an imaginary kingdom, Gondal (*LP*, 19)—critics make inferences from *Wuthering Heights* which are of course speculative. However little we know about her, we can be sure that Emily Brontë would resent the assumption that her reclusiveness and her absorption in an imaginary world precluded concern for the outside world. Choosing to be marginal is not the same as choosing to escape from reality. Brontë cannot have been unaware of the political and social implications of *Wuthering Heights,* which explores the positive value of social, personal, and literary marginality. We shall see that Catherine's diary, written in the margins of the sacred and revered texts of her culture, is paradigmatic of *Wuthering Heights* itself (62). The writing in the margin effects a subversion of repressive Victorian ideology. Brontë's own personal writings resemble Catherine's in being secretive, miniscule, and marginal;[4] but, like Catherine's, Brontë's writing was clearly both powerful and liberating.

Probably the experience of teaching (which she loathed) sensitized Emily to social hierarchy and marginality. Female teachers, like governesses, were an embarrassment to Victorian society, being educated middle-class young women forced into the "unladylike" position of having to earn a living.[5] Emily was exploited by her employers: "This is slavery. I fear she will never stand it," said Charlotte, and sure enough, the hard work and long hours gave Emily a physical and mental breakdown (*JB*, 294, 306).

In an increasingly stratified society, the Brontës were strangely anomalous; though middle-class by virtue of their father's profession in the Church, they could also be considered working-class by virtue of his Irish peasant origin, and the family remained poor. In nineteenth-century England, the rising middle-class defined itself against all others: one's class and economic position in the social hierarchy were thought to indicate one's morality. Henry Mayhew's famous *London Labour and the London Poor* (1861–62) categorized individuals on a social and ethical spectrum. *Wuthering Heights* draws on Victorian analogies between the body, the social body, and urban location.[6] The typical Victorian middle-class home, for example, was divided between an "upstairs" and a "downstairs" which referred to the people as well as the places, and was also implicitly modelled on the body: the servants "lived in . . . the 'back passages' (nursery euphemism for anus)"; they took care of bodies and waste matter, leaving those who inhabited the "upstairs" free for "higher" pursuits.[7] In the Brontë household the division of labor was less rigid—Emily baked bread while studying—but domestic chores were performed by the women. Middle-class Victorians also saw the home as the extension of the woman herself, a belief which Brontë uses ironically in *Wuthering Heights* to expose women's vulnerability.[8] Brontë's novel can be said to be entirely set in the "back passages"; the first reviewers certainly thought not only that it described those who were socially marginal and geographically remote, but also that the author had "drag[ged] into light" all that was "coarse and loathsome, in his wanderings" (see chap. 3).[9] Brontë's interest in "the peasantry amongst whom she lived" is explained by Charlotte as akin to Wordsworth's interest in "rustic" life (38). It would be more accurate to see *Wuthering Heights* as a corrective to Wordsworth's romantic belief that "the essential passions of the heart find a better soil" in the country, since it shows that such passions may be destructive.[10]

Heathcliff, the most anti-social character in *Wuthering Heights*, could well have been influenced by Byron's anti-heroes, although he outdoes "the Byronic hero in his romantic rebellion."[11] His obsessive quest for Catherine resembles religious fanaticism, and could have been suggested by "mad Methodist magazines, full of miracles and apparitions and preternatural warnings."[12] Aunt Branwell, who raised the Brontës, espoused a Calvinism which Emily satirizes in Joseph, although she also secularizes the intense emotionalism of the religion.[13] If Heathcliff's self-willed death echoes an incident in John Wesley's *Journals,* his exhuming Catherine's corpse echoes "The Bridegroom of Barna," one of many stories involving violence and the supernatural in *Blackwood's Magazine* which Emily read.[14] The Byronic hero, combined with the setting in the historic past, and the narrative style of Brontë's novel may suggest the influence of Walter Scott, whom Emily greatly admired (*JB*, 152).[15] Brontë extends Scott's modification of the Gothic genre by employing a horror-story for psychological purposes; she "modernises and domesticates Gothic" by making it credible (*LP*, 24).

Wuthering Heights assimilates the elements of Gothic—violence, revenge, omens, ghosts, and even necrophilia—into a realistic story of the lives of two Yorkshire families. However absorbed Emily may have been in her imagination, she lived in the center of the woolen and cotton producing district of England, and could not have avoided the sight of thousands of people, unemployed because of the new technology, "drifting, destitute and often starving, into the villages and towns."[16] Heathcliff, plucked from the streets of Liverpool, could well, says Terry Eagleton, be an Irish immigrant, "but by no means certainly. Heathcliff may be a gypsy, or (like Bertha Mason in *Jane Eyre*) a Creole, or any kind of alien. It is hard to know how black he is."[17] Christopher Heywood believes that Heathcliff is Jamaican and that *Wuthering Heights* is an Abolitionist satire of families living in the Yorkshire Dales whose fortunes were made in sugar plantations.[18] In light of Marx and Engles's *Communist Manifesto* (published three years after Brontë's novel), Heathcliff has been seen as a working-class hero who uses the capitalist weapons of his oppressors—"money and arranged marriages"—against them.[19]

Although Heathcliff chooses exile to resist oppression on the grounds of his race and class, he in turn, by virtue of his gender, is given the power to oppress others. The primary concern of *Wuthering Heights* is neither racism nor capitalism but patriarchy. In 1847, when *Wuthering Heights* was published, women and children were the legal property of their husbands, a law which Heathcliff exploits to wreak his revenge. By 1847, wife abuse was a daily feature of the newspapers which Emily read.[20] Brontë's novel, like her sister Anne's *The Tenant of Wildfell Hall*, depicts men's abuse of women. *Wuthering Heights* can thus be compared to "social problem" novels such as Elizabeth Gaskell's *Mary Barton* (1848) or Charles Dickens's *Oliver Twist* (1838).

The most truly marginal character in *Wuthering Heights* is Catherine. She speaks to us directly only from the margins of a "tome," and exists as a ghost for most of the novel (62). A ghost is the most liminal figure that we can conceive, being neither dead nor alive, neither of this world nor the other. In the ghostly figure of Catherine, Emily Brontë employs a Gothic motif for ideological purposes. Catherine's ghost attests to her oppression by patriarchy (she dies as a result of a male contest to possess her) but also shows that she refuses to be supressed. Thus Brontë's renowned fascination with the supernatural, whether derived from the Gothic, or Methodism, or traditional ballads (another popular, and predominantly oral form), is consistent with what I perceive as her interest in marginality, whether social, existential, or literary.[21] Even the genres which she seems to have preferred were "mass" rather than "high" culture. Vereen Bell argues that *Wuthering Heights* should be seen as part of an oral tradition, meant to be heard and not read.[22] Certainly, in straddling Gothic and realistic genres, *Wuthering Heights* is a borderline or threshold work. Catherine's writing in the margin and her ghostliness resemble Brontë's. If her absence from *Wuthering Heights* paradoxically makes her powerfully present throughout, the same can be said of Emily Brontë's place in literary history.

2

The Importance of the Work

Tracing possible influences on *Wuthering Heights* does little to explain it. There is no work in the canon of English literature which is quite so disconcerting: it upsets our expectations and beliefs about the nature of the novel, of love, and even of human identity. Some years ago, when my sister urged me to read *Wuthering Heights,* she said it was one of the greatest love stories ever written. I do not think she would say that now. I remember being very puzzled (as were the first reviewers in 1847) about how to react: was this a love story? who in the novel could I trust? was this realism or fantasy? If it were intended as a story about the everyday life of ordinary people, what about the ghosts? My questions, and the confusion they revealed, were precisely what makes *Wuthering Heights* an important and unique work in the history of English Literature.

Wuthering Heights seems to stand alone in the literary tradition; it is very difficult to write about its links to past works or its influence on other works and authors. This is because it upsets our understanding of what the novel should be. As we saw in the previous chapter, *Wuthering Heights* spans the very different genres of Gothic and domestic fiction. Finding a point of view on the story is difficult: there are two narrators whose versions of events are often indistinguishable, and who both seem increasingly unreliable. The characters in the novel are similarly elusive. The book opens with confusion about the identities of the inhabitants of the Heights; although their natures are disclosed as the novel progresses, we end the book feeling that the mystery has not been dispelled. Furthermore, there doesn't seem to be a tangible moral to the story: the appearance of the ghosts at the beginning and end seems to preclude the fulfillment of an obvious message. The existence of the ghosts also perplexes us about whether this is a realistic account of working people in a Yorkshire village or a work of rather grotesque fantasy. *Wuthering Heights,* then, leaves us in dismay about our customary ways of reading.

It is this power to disconcert and agitate which made *Wuthering Heights* notorious when it was first published in 1847, and which makes it so exciting and exhilarating today. This peculiarly engimatic novel has drawn critics of every possible school of thinking to try to explain it, but they can't. As J. Hillis Miller has observed, there is always something left over, something "just at the edge of the circle of theoretical vision" that eludes explanation.[1] There has been (as we shall see) a plethora of diagrams and visual aids in critical studies of *Wuthering Heights;* it is as though critics cannot resist trying to control and contain a disturbing and, it seems, threatening novel.

People have experimented with alternative ways to interpret or come to terms with *Wuthering Heights:* there are movie versions, songs, parodies, and fictional supplements, all of which attest to the immense fascination of the novel.[2] There is perhaps no literary work that has so taken hold of what is usually referred to as the "popular imagination." The novel has been important to generations of non-academic readers: my sister read the novel because our mother recommended it and mum read it because her grandmother recommended it.

For most people, the mere mention of *Wuthering Heights* conjures up an image of a wind-swept heath, with two outcast lovers passionately embracing. However, what makes the novel important to us now is that it forces us to question why readers have been, and still are, willing to regard the relationship between Heathcliff and Catherine as one of love.[3] The novel is also, as one of my students once said, "all about hate." It offers a striking demonstration of how patriarchal ideology can issue in the abuse of women and children, and, more importantly, it demonstrates women's creative ways of resisting oppression. Most remarkable, perhaps, is the strangely modern insight offered by *Wuthering Heights* into what we now call "gendered ways of knowing."

Surprisingly, the domestic violence in *Wuthering Heights* has been almost entirely ignored; perhaps this is because readers are distracted by the intensity of Heathcliff's passion, which they want to perceive as "love."[4] There is certainly a strong erotic aspect to the emotions and experiences in *Wuthering Heights* though this does not necessarily make them those of love. To put it bluntly, I can think of no other nineteenth-century novel which talks so much about sex, and which disturbingly links sex to violence. This implicit sexual dimension is, I believe, what David Musselwhite calls the "unacceptable text" in *Wuthering Heights*.[5] When Musselwhite describes the "unread and outcast text" which has "remained to haunt and trouble the cosiness of conventional readings, tapping, like the waif Catherine, on a shuttered consciousness," he points to the thematic significance of Catherine's ghost (*DM*, 155).

What makes Brontë's novel so troubling and yet baffling is, perhaps, this specter of violence, and what makes it so appealing is its affirmation of survival: the ambiguity is embodied in Catherine's ghost. Certainly, the power to deeply disturb constitutes what is called the "greatness" of *Wuthering Heights*. In order to open the shutters of our consciousness, it seems, we must let Catherine in.

3

Critical Reception

By far the most influential critic of *Wuthering Heights* is Charlotte Brontë, who in 1850, while grieving for her sister Emily, wrote a Preface and Biographical Notice to the second edition of the novel (30–41). Charlotte's analysis defined the scope of all future criticism, which has taken the form of an implicit debate about whether *Wuthering Heights* is social commentary and authentic realism, or imaginative outpouring and mystical vision. These mutually exclusive explanations both find their justification, surprisingly, in Charlotte Brontë's assertion that *Wuthering Heights* is "rooted" in the Yorkshire moors:

> *Wuthering Heights* . . . is rustic all through. It is moorish, and wild, and knotty as the root of heath. Nor was it natural that it should be otherwise; the author being herself a native and nursling of the moors. (38)

By arguing that *Wuthering Heights* was the "natural" product of someone living on the moors, Charlotte opened the critical debate about whether the "moorishness" of *Wuthering Heights* refers to the external reality of Brontë's surroundings or the internal quality of her mind.

The Preface seems to offer conflicting accounts of *Wuthering Heights* (*HM*, 48). But Charlotte was defending her sister's name on all sides from hostile reviews, especially from prejudices about her provincialism and her gender. The reviews of *Wuthering Heights* made Emily Brontë seem culturally marginal. Charlotte responds by deliberately confusing the implicit binaries in the criticism that made Emily seem unlettered, unfeminine, and unconscious in her art. The first critics of *Wuthering Heights* were struck above all by its violence and brutality (*CH*, 240, 228, 231, 234). Anxious about publicly declaring for the first time that such a violent novel had been written by a woman, Charlotte presented her sister as a unique blend of feminine piety and masculine creative power; an artist who combines hard labor with mystical inspiration.

The reviewers were bewildered by *Wuthering Heights*: "We are not aware," said one critic in dismay, "that anything has been written upon the rank that ought to be assigned to such works as *Wuthering Heights*" (*CH*, 241). One critic declared that: "It should have been called *Withering Heights*, for any thing from which the mind and body would more instinctively shrink . . . cannot be easily imagined" (*CH*, 229). To explain the disturbing aspects of the novel, its setting was seized upon: on the Yorkshire moors apparently, "human beings, like the trees, grow gnarled and dwarfed and distorted by the inclement climate" (*CH*, 218). Once the remoteness of the region explains the "savages" (*CH*, 220) in the novel, the novel itself is said to display "rugged power—an unconscious strength" "so rude, so unfinished and so careless" (*CH*, 230, 226). Then the "misshapen" characters and the "disjointed" novel are assumed to proceed from the "rough shaggy uncouth power" of the artist herself (or rather himself); Emily Brontë is rendered as weird and marginal as the characters she creates (*CH*, 224, 220, 234). In concluding that *Wuthering Heights* must be the product of an unlettered mind, the critics placed it outside of the province of art by the same gesture that placed its characters outside of civilized society.

Charlotte Brontë seems to affirm Emily Brontë's marginality when she depicts her in the Preface as "a native and nursling of the moors," unaccustomed "to what is called 'the world'" (38). Charlotte's expression of sympathy with readers who find the characters in their "remote and unreclaimed region" "repulsive" is, however, a clever tactic to undermine their prejudices (38, 37). She goes on to say that "men and women who,"

> with feelings moderate in degree, and little marked in kind, have been trained from their cradle to observe the utmost evenness of manner and guardedness of language, will hardly know what to make of the rough, strong utterance, the harshly manifested passions, the unbridled aversions, and headlong partialities of unlettered moorland hinds and rugged moorland squires. (37)

Brontë makes the "unlettered moorland hinds" with their strong passions superior to "educated society"; those who are repulsed by *Wuthering Heights* must have shallow ("moderate") feelings and superficial ("artificial") tastes. Complaints about the "vivid and fearful scenes," were, says Charlotte, met by Emily with charges of "affectation" (39). Charlotte defends the offensive language of the novel by declaring the convention of replacing certain words with blanks to be hypocritical: "I cannot tell what good it does—what feeling it spares—what horror it conceals" (38).

The Preface claims that the strong and brutal passions and harsh language of *Wuthering Heights* are the product of a pious and retiring young woman. Emily Brontë apparently lived like a nun:

> My sister's disposition was not naturally gregarious; circumstances favoured and fostered her tendency to seclusion; except to go to church or take a walk on the hills, she rarely crossed the threshold of home. (38)

This ideal (and irreproachable) Victorian woman, however, hid a masculine power:

> Under an unsophisticated culture, inartificial tastes, and an unpretending outside, lay a secret power and fire that might have informed the brain and kindled the veins of a hero. (35)

As well as calling Emily a "hero," and a "he," Charlotte continues to use the pseudonym "Ellis Bell." This effects a clear distinction between the private woman and the public artist, which enables Charlotte to argue that although Emily Brontë produced a vigorous (masculine) novel she remained an ideally feminine woman. Her poems are described as not "at all like the poetry women generally write," being "condensed and terse, vigorous and genuine" (30–31). In presenting her sister as a combination of "the extremes of vigour and simplicity," Charlotte preserves the gender ambiguity of the Brontës' pseudonyms. Emily combined typically 'masculine' and 'feminine' qualities: "Stronger than a man, simpler than a child, her nature stood alone" (35).

The Preface offers two contradictory explanations of the power or genius behind *Wuthering Heights*. Critics ever since have echoed one or the other, but what they haven't noticed is the gendered nature of the descriptions. Charlotte characterizes her sister's creative power as masculine in an extended metaphor taken from an early review (one of five found in Emily's desk) (*CH*, 226):

> *Wuthering Heights* was hewn in a wild workshop, with simple tools, out of homely materials. The statuary found a granite block on a solitary moor: gazing thereon, he saw how from the crag might be elicited the head, savage, swart, sinister; a form moulded with at least one element of grandeur—power. He wrought with a rude chisel, and from no model but the vision of his meditations. With time and labour, the crag took human shape; and there it stands colossal, dark, and frowning, half-statue, half rock. . . . (41)

This image of a virile and potent muse laboring on rugged raw materials emphasizes the painstaking craft that produced *Wuthering Heights*. But this is immediately preceded in the Preface with a contradictory image of Emily Brontë in a typically feminine role as "the nominal artist" working "passively under dictates [she] neither delivered nor could question" (41):

> The writer who possesses the creative gift owns something of which he is not always master—something that at times strangely wills and works for itself. (40)

14

Charlotte Brontë's 1850 Preface and Biographical Notice implicitly absolve her sister of responsibility for her own creation: she cannot be blamed for recording a brutal reality, neither can she be blamed for her powerful inspiration. From this point on critics would be divided over whether *Wuthering Heights* is realistic or allegorical, a reflection of the real lives of people in a remote region, or a product of a mystical vision.

The 1850 Preface did not, as Melvin Watson observes, provoke "any more understanding" of *Wuthering Heights*.[1] It took fifty years to allay the charges of coarseness, and much longer to dispel the myth of the accidental artist. Swinburne's 1883 essay vindicated the novel's violence by emphasizing its "noble purity and passionate straightforwardness." His defense effected a turn towards seeing it as a love story, but he also claimed that the love between Catherine and Heathcliff was an "ardent chastity," a passion of souls.[2] In 1990, Peter Miles tellingly entitles a chapter on critical reactions to Catherine and Heathcliff: "Writing/Erasing/Reading Sexuality" (*PM*, 35), referring to the denial of the sexual dimension in *Wuthering Heights*.

Swinburne's claim that the passion in *Wuthering Heights* is not physical but mystical nourished the conception of Emily Brontë as a romantic artist which has, in various guises, persisted until today. Although in 1926 C.P. Sanger demonstrated Emily Brontë's knowledge of inheritance law, and the minutely accurate chronology of the plot of *Wuthering Heights,* he did not manage to dispel the view that it was "nominal" or accidental.[3] The deliberate and careful craft of the novel was assimilated to a romantic interpretation by making *Wuthering Heights* a dramatization of spiritual forces. In 1934 Cecil commended Emily Brontë's artistry, but insisted that she was nevertheless a "mystic," and *Wuthering Heights* is an allegory of "transcendental reality." The cosmos, in Emily Brontë's philosophy, is a harmony between the conflicting forces, or principles, of calm and storm, and Catherine and Heathcliff are children of the storm.[4] Dorothy Van Ghent, in 1953, also argues that Cathy and Heathcliff are "portions of the flux of nature, children of rock and heath and tempest," but she extends the mythical explanation of the novel into an early version of psychological interpretation.[5] In this view the novel is still an allegory of elemental forces (early views of the novel's "savagery" persist), but they are now located in the psyche. Emily Brontë as "the nominal artist" persists in psychoanalytic interpretations of the novel.

Psychoanalytic critics also discovered the probably unintended theme of incest in the novel;[6] and Thomas Moser, in "What Is the Matter with Emily Jane?," claims that Emily Brontë did not realize that *Wuthering Heights* is all about sex.[7] Although condescending, the argument has its source in Charlotte's assertion that Emily didn't know what she was doing when she created Heathcliff (40). Moser replaces Charlotte's explanation of Heathcliff as the embodiment of evil with Heathcliff as the embodiment of the id:

> The primary traits which Freud ascribed to the id apply perfectly to Heathcliff: the source of psychic energy; the seat of the instincts (particularly sex and death); the essence of dreams; the archaic foundation of personality—selfish, asocial, impulsive. (*TM*, 4)

Psychoanalytic criticism combines with close reading in Van de Laar's impressive cataloguing of imagery. *The Inner Structure Of Wuthering Heights* refers not only to the novel but also to the structure of the mind, so that once again the deliberate artist is assimilated into the spontaneous one.[8]

The psychoanalytic approach did not free itself from Charlotte Brontë's "nominal" artist until James Kavanagh's 1985 reading. Although Kavanagh argues, like Van Ghent thirty years previously, that *Wuthering Heights* functions like a dream, and that the cruelty and sadism in the novel are compensation for repressed libidinal desire, he sees the representation of psychological conflict as symptomatic of the social tensions created by capitalism. Thus Kavanagh makes the psychoanalytic approach compatible with a cultural materialist analysis of the social circumstances of *Wuthering Heights*.[9]

The sociological or historical approach to *Wuthering Heights* was slower to develop, and hounded by romanticism. David Wilson's 1947 essay pioneered readings which sought to "restore a more realistic sense of the socio-historical conjuncture in which Emily Brontë lived and wrote" (*JK*, 7). Wilson saw *Wuthering Heights* as a dramatization of social rather than cosmic or psychological conflict. Emily Brontë, in his view, confronted:

> On the one hand, cruelty accompanied by the hypocritical religion and morality of an old culture; on the other hand, a youthful power, having the spark of life, yet dark, uncouth, uncivilised, and potent with hate and destruction (*DW*, 108).

Even this determinedly sociological reading, however, tends to mythicize *Wuthering Heights* as "a struggle between two forces, each in some ways evil" (*DW*, 108). Terry Eagleton's 1975 Marxist reading admits that *Wuthering Heights* is myth—"apparently timeless, highly integrated, mysteriously autonomous"—but points out that "such a notion of myth is itself . . . ideologically based."[10] Eagleton nevertheless mythicizes the novel when he places Catherine and Heathcliff "outside the family and society into an opposing realm which can be adequately imaged only as 'Nature'" (*TE*, 103). In 1977, Musselwhite declared that Marxist criticism of *Wuthering Heights* has differed little from that of the liberal tradition which turns the novel into an "acceptable text," perpetuating the status quo (*DM*, 155).

The most explicit opponents of Emily Brontë as a "nominal" or accidental artist have been feminist critics who see such characterizations as one of the many ways in which art by women is devalued.[11] Feminist criticism, in line with the sociological side of the critical debate we are charting, traditionally emphasizes the realistic, rather than the mystical, aspect of the novel. Like the Marxists, however, some feminist critics are bemused by *Wuthering Heights,* perhaps because it seems to resist an exclusive focus on gender. Inga-Stina Ewbank's first full-length study of the Brontës as female novelists, in 1966, has great difficulty fitting Emily Brontë into its exploration of how the sisters dealt with Victorian notions of women's "proper sphere." "There is no evidence in Emily's work," says Ewbank, of concern for her position as a woman, but rather for the "profound and incurable" frustrations "of the human condition."[12] Like Ewbank, Sandra Gilbert and Susan Gubar, in 1978, have some difficulty fitting Emily Brontë into their reading of nineteenth-century female novelists' anxiety about entering a male tradition: they devote only sixty pages to Emily compared to one hundred and twenty-nine for Charlotte.[13]

Lyn Pykett, however, has more recently (1989) argued that *Wuthering Heights* is an explicitly feminist work which dramatizes and exposes the Victorian doctrine of separate spheres so oppressive to women: "the masculine world of hard work and the physical battle with nature at the Heights," is opposed to "the feminine world of luxury, leisure, culture and the domestic ideal at the Grange" (*LP,* 111). Pykett argues, in opposition to Gilbert and Gubar who see Heathcliff as "female" (*G&G,* 294) that "all of the male characters in this novel are clearly associated with authority and/or oppression" (*LP,* 110). Peter Miles, in 1990, agrees that "Woman is shown as the front-line victim of human sexuality," while male sexuality is presented as "problematical" (*PM,* 39, 42). Attesting to its importance for women readers, *Wuthering Heights* is chosen in a recent book (*Feminist Readings/Feminists Reading*) for three of six chapters employing a variety of feminist approaches (*F/R,* 79).

John Allen Stevenson's essay on the "Question of Likeness in *Wuthering Heights,*" inadvertently contributes to feminist readings of *Wuthering Heights* by arguing that Heathcliff is not the central figure of the novel. Heathcliff's statement "I cannot live without my love," is intended quite literally, he says, because Heathcliff's very being originates in Catherine.[14] With this claim that Heathcliff's self is somehow centered outside of himself, Stevenson anticipates poststructuralist approaches to Brontë's novel.

It is the "ontological slipperiness" in the novel which attracts poststructuralist criticism.[15] Leo Bersani, in 1978, argued that *Wuthering Heights* dramatizes "frenetic uncertainty about the very possibility of being" (*LB,* 190). This approach, which emphasizes the constructed and divided nature of subjectivity, can be seen as a later development of the mythical school of *Wuthering Heights* criticism. In *The Disappearance of God* (1964), Hillis Miller typifies the religious interpretations of the work when he sees *Wuthering Heights* as representing Emily Brontë's conviction that "a person is most himself when he participates most completely in the life of something

outside himself."[16] It is a fairly short leap to John Matthew's typically poststructuralist claim that the novel's "passion involves a
yearning for self-possession by means of the passage through the
other."[17] By 1982, Hillis Miller subscribes to the view that there is
no unity of either self or story in *Wuthering Heights* (*HM,* 512); and
John Matthews goes so far as to claim that *Wuthering Heights* makes
explicit that "story" is "the only mode of being": the characters, like
all of us, have "being" or subjectivity only by virtue of being framed
by narrative (*JM,* 28).

So far we have seen that although critics of *Wuthering Heights*
subscribe to widely different schools of theory, there is a fairly clear
division between those who emphasize the realism and those who
emphasize the romanticism of the novel. The best of the most recent
criticism however, like Kavanagh's psychoanalytic-cultural materialist
analysis discussed above, is theoretically eclectic. One of the most useful single works on *Wuthering Heights,* part of the *Case Studies in
Contemporary Criticism* series, offers essays employing five of the
dominant approaches to the text (Psychoanalytic, Feminist, Decon-
tructionist, Marxist, and Cultural Critical) and also gives a very useful
introduction to each theory.[18] Nancy Armstrong's contribution,
"Imperialist Nostalgia and *Wuthering Heights,*" argues that *Wuthering
Heights* was part of a general process of internal cultural colonization
in Britain, whereby certain regions and their inhabitants were rendered marginal, "exotic and backward" (*CS,* 432). Armstrong sees
Charlotte Brontë's Preface and Biographical Notice as tying Emily
Brontë to "nature, to a region, and to a regional dialect" (*CS,* 440),
thus ensuring that both author and novel "would be received with the
same appetite that Victorians brought to accounts of native customs
and collections of antiquities" (*CS,* 440).

Whereas Armstrong's essay leaves ambiguous Emily Brontë's
role in "imperialist nostalgia," Christopher Heywood's painstaking
historical essay on Brontë's "Yorkshire background" (1993), combined with an earlier account of "Yorkshire Slavery in *Wuthering
Heights*" (1987), suggest that Brontë's novel is a strong indictment
of the involvement of a group of local families in Jamaican sugar

plantations: "She read their history, it appears, as an example of the extinction of yeoman strength under the enervating and brutalizing influence of the Caribbean sugar economy" (*YB*, 819).

Heywood sees Brontë's attack on slavery as implying an analogy with women's oppression (*YB*, 820). *Wuthering Heights*' analysis of women's objectification under patriarchy is nowhere better analyzed than in Beth Newman's 1990 essay, which offers a feminist psychoanalytic exploration of the gaze in *Wuthering Heights* within a broader analysis of the role of visual metaphors in critical vocabulary.[19] Newman's essay, which has been influential in my own reading of the novel, shows how the male gaze in *Wuthering Heights* attempts to dominate women, but also how the novel offers a feminist resistance to the patriarchal gaze.

The myriad of interpretations of *Wuthering Heights* are all, says Hillis Miller, partially right and partially wrong: "The error lies in the assumption that the meaning is going to be single, unified, and logically coherent" (*HM*, 51). The "best readings," he says, bringing us full circle, are those "like Charlotte Brontë's, which repeat in their own logic the text's failure to satisfy the mind's desire for logical order with a demonstrable base" (*HM*, 53). Charlotte's Preface, in other words, with its contradictory explanations, mirrors the lack of a unified meaning in *Wuthering Heights* itself. We shall see in chapter 11, A Warning About Visual Aids! that the elusive nature of *Wuthering Heights* makes critics very anxious.

A READING

4

Wuthering Heights:
The Writing in the Margin

Wuthering Heights is often interpreted in spatial terms: Thrushcross Grange is contrasted to Wuthering Heights, as inside is to outside, and culture is to nature.[1] Spatial locations have particular emotional or psychological connotations: the security and warmth of the hearth, for example, is quite different from the exhilaration and trepidation felt in an open space. In *Wuthering Heights* the most important location is neither inside nor outside, but that highly-charged and ambiguous space in between. As Van de Laar observes, thresholds in *Wuthering Heights* convey openness, power, freedom and life, as well as closeness, inferiority, imprisonment and death (*VL*, 107–55). Her examination of the imagery of the novel lists 312 instances in which windows, doors, gates, and other passageways are significant. If we add the recesses of the Heights where the dogs lurk (47, 49), or the corners where the children cower (63), then the examples become even more numerous. Many key events in *Wuthering Heights* take place, as we shall see, in marginal spaces such as the back-kitchen, the garden, the moors, or near the open window. In most readers' minds, *Wuthering Heights* is associated with the moors—a liminal space which seems to transcend time and space. Surprisingly, the heath is not actually featured very much, although it does represent the very spirit and essence of the novel, which is concerned above all with margins: with social, personal, and literary boundaries.

Perhaps the most important marginal space in *Wuthering Heights* is Catherine's diary which is written in the blank spaces of the tomes perused by Lockwood. When readers enter the story of *Wuthering Heights* through Catherine's marginalia, we are also introduced to the major tropes of the novel. Catherine's diary combines a strong visual image of her social marginalization with an exploration of writing and reading as acts of resistance. The diary defaces the "tome(s)" and "Testament(s)" from which as a child Catherine is forced to learn the correct behavior and the conventional values of her society (62). Although locating her writing in the margins of revered texts could be said to reveal Catherine's repression by patriarchal society, it also represents her rebellion. The "writing in the margin," we shall see, is an embodiment of Catherine's ghost: the spirit of female resistance which will not be extinguished.

Catherine's diary, especially the form that it takes, offers keys to understanding *Wuthering Heights*. All of the characters in the novel are implicitly placed in relation to a moral center and a margin, conveyed as much by their habitual or preferred physical locations as by their espoused views. To put it very briefly, Lockwood, Joseph, Nelly, and Edgar Linton prefer to be "inside" of institutions and conventions, while Catherine, Heathcliff, and Cathy deliberately place themselves "outside" of social norms. In general, those who advocate conventional morality use it to repress others. Heathcliff is the exception because, although he is socially marginalized, he remains entrenched in patriarchal values and so—like Joseph, Lockwood, and Edgar— attempts to control women.

Joseph, at the center of the Heights, represents and embodies the restrictive and sexist norms of Victorian society. Joseph remains "beside the hearth," and shows a great preference "for locked doors and gates" (*VL*, 239). Nelly is always around doors and windows, policing the borders of "normalcy." If Nelly is "patriarchy's . . . housekeeper" (*G&G*, 290–91), her loyalty is to Edgar Linton who never seems to move beyond Thrushcross Grange, and who tries to prevent Catherine and especially his daughter Cathy from doing so. Those on the "inside" generally battle to keep loved-ones in (Nelly, for example, tries to keep the window closed when Catherine is dying) and to keep others out.

On the other hand are those characters who seek exits and entrances. Lockwood, though highly conventional, is always attempting to barge into resisting barriers, whether it is the gate at the Heights, Catherine's bed-closet, the window, or the covers of Catherine's books (although the Heights resists, even to the end of the novel, his attempts to penetrate it). Catherine is seen pleading at the beginning to be "let . . . in" to the Heights (67); although she is already dead when the novel opens, and dies only a third of the way through the inner story, she seems to haunt the text, always hovering at its margins. Although he meets less resistance, Heathcliff, like Lockwood, is given to bursting through barriers, particularly when he returns from his three-year absence.

The house as a symbol of social institutions and conventional values is complicated, however, by its deeper meaning. *Wuthering Heights* employs the Victorian view of the home as an extension of the woman for ironic purposes. The house is unconsciously for the men equivalent to the female body, both of which they seek to appropriate. Lockwood's and Heathcliff's violations of space imply, we shall see, sexual violations. *Wuthering Heights* dramatizes a struggle between men for ownership of two families' houses and women. When Edgar and Heathcliff finally confront one another at the hearth in the kitchen of the Grange, they battle not only for possession of the territory but also for possession of Catherine (152–55).

All three of the major female characters—Catherine, Nelly, and Cathy—are associated at some key point with another variant on the home: the motif of the nest (147, 160, 259). The nest, as Gaston Bachelard describes, is an archetypally female image:

> "I had just discovered the feminine significance of a nest set in the fork of two branches. The thicket took on such a human quality that I called out: "Don't touch it, above all don't touch it!"[2]

Bachelard recognizes that although the nest "sets us to daydreaming of security," it is "a precarious thing" (*GB,* 102). In *Wuthering Heights* the nest, identified with the women, appears only as despoiled and devastated: personal integrity (both physical and mental) is, especially for the women, continually threatened. The emphasis on the vulnerability of thresholds in *Wuthering Heights* betrays anxiety about personal physical boundaries.

If the male characters in *Wuthering Heights* unconsciously associate houses with women, they also unconsciously associate women with texts. The link is perhaps not surprising. Patriarchal society, says the anthropologist Claude Levi-Strauss, functions by exchanging women between groups of men.[3] When women are exchanged as objects, they also function, says Levi-Strauss, as signs—that is, they become symbols, documents of the exchange itself (*L-S,* 496). Heathcliff's revenge against the Lintons involves stealing their women, Catherine, Isabella, and Cathy. He then quite literally marks the women with signs of his ownership in the form of bruises and cuts. Heathcliff's violence is presented as an act of inscription by which he turns women into texts (see chap. 7). Lockwood, on the other hand, sees the text as a woman. His violation of the privacy of Catherine's diary is presented in sexual terms, as a substitute for penetrating Cathy. But Lockwood is impotent as a reader and a lover: his famous nightmares combine fear of sex with fear of the text (see chap. 5). The men in *Wuthering Heights* fear feminine sexuality which becomes associated with a similarly threatening textuality. Joseph despoils his sacred texts: he "ransaks" the Bible for "curses" to "fling" at others, particularly the women (see chap. 6).

This "phallocentric" approach to texts, which is centered on and protective of male power and domination, is exhibited by all those— Nelly, Joseph, Lockwood, Edgar, Heathcliff, and Hareton—who also oppress and coerce women. It is contrasted to the "feminine" reading and writing strategies practiced by Catherine and Cathy and exemplified in Catherine's diary (see chaps. 5, 8, 10). Rather than attempting to penetrate and violently rend the "Testament," Catherine seeks to engulf it in her own writing, giving voice to the femininity repressed by phallocentric discourse. Filling in the blanks in the "dominant discourse," which espouses the values of the status quo, is precisely the strategy advocated by the French feminist Luce Irigaray to subvert patriarchy.[4] Catherine's writing in the margin thus goes far beyond defacing a particular "tome": it represents a subversion of the values which the conventional characters embody, as well as resistance to sexual domination. Catherine's challenge to phallocentrism is taken up by her daughter Cathy (see chap. 10), and implicitly of course by Emily Brontë herself.

Wuthering Heights, as more than one critic has noticed, "is 'about' reading" and writing (*DM,* 155). More importantly, it is about the relationship between the way we read and the way we treat and view others. All the major characters in the novel (with the exception of Nelly) exhibit specific attitudes to texts which are linked to their gender. *Wuthering Heights* presents reading as a sublimation of sexual desire. The text, like the house, presents borders which invite yet resist penetration. The entrances into a house, a body and a text, are all, as Mary Douglas claims, susceptible to violation: "Any structure of ideas is vulnerable at its margins. We should expect the orifices of the body to symbolize its specially vulnerable points."[5] The impact of *Wuthering Heights* depends on readers' tendency (as Peter Stallybrass and Allon White have discussed) to visualize the mind, the body, the social body (and I would add the body of the text) in parallel ways (*S&W,* 2–3). The novel relies on analogies between domestic, bodily and textual spaces, and especially on our anxiety about margins. But we shall see that the writing in the margin in *Wuthering Heights* is a powerful subversive force.

5

Entering the Heights:
Lockwood, and Catherine's Diary

The opening pages of *Wuthering Heights* show "Lockwood's ushering of the reader into . . . the innermost imaginary recesses of Emily Brontë's text" (*JK*, 26). Lockwood is generally regarded by critics as the surrogate reader in *Wuthering Heights*:

> Lockwood acts as the reader's prime agent. His initial willingness to partake of a reality peopled by characters totally alien to his previous experience becomes congruous with that of any reader who ventures into the book.[1]

Although this overestimates Lockwood's ability to embrace the experience offered by the Heights, it is significant that both of the above critics imply that Lockwood is engaged in a venture, shared by the reader, into a potentially frightening space. These critics, probably unintentionally, reveal the sexual nature of Lockwood's determination, in the opening pages of the novel, to enter a space which resists penetration. The reader is potentially engaged in a violation.

Lockwood's first visit to the Heights, described in the opening sentences, is an unwelcome intrusion; although Heathcliff tells Lockwood to "walk in," it is through "closed teeth," and expresses "the sentiment 'Go to the Deuce'" (45). Heathcliff can hardly ignore Lockwood's horse "fairly pushing the barrier," so he "sullenly" "unchain[s]" it (45). There are, Van de Laar has demonstrated, a great number of images of apertures associated with Lockwood in *Wuthering Heights,* which "express symbolically the idea of penetration into an otherwise enclosed space" (*VL,* 107). The sexual connotations of Lockwood's penetration into the Heights are unmistakable, and we shall see that they intensify throughout the first four chapters until they reach a climax with the vision of Catherine's ghost.

Once inside the "penetralium" of the Heights, Lockwood remarks with some pride that "its entire anatomy" is "laid bare to an inquiring eye" (46, 47). The "anatomy" of this home, however, disturbs Lockwood. It is not the conventional feminine space that the Victorians (as we saw in chap. 4) expected home to be. The hearth, that cozy heart of domesticity closely associated with the woman, is here utilitarian and even aggressive: "Above the chimney were sundry villainous old guns, and a couple of horse-pistols" (47). Clearly, the Heights is not a haven from a hostile world, but a part of that world. The dogs which "haunt" the "recesses" exhibit the violent spirit of the house: as Heathcliff so rightly points out of the one that attacks Lockwood, "she's not accustomed to be spoiled—not kept for a pet" (48). The same can be said for the women in this house.[2] It is as though this home has no loving feminine influence: people subsist on porridge, and Cathy takes part in the ritual of tea-time only under duress (53). The Heights as a domestic space is disturbingly unfeminine.

In fact, in the Heights Lockwood enters a grotesque twilight zone where his perceptions are confused. The lack of an "introductory lobby or passageway," would have been especially significant to the Victorians, for whom a lack of distinctions between inside and outside carried over into social categories (46). The bourgeois Victorian horror of working-class culture was due to what they called a lack of "separation." James Shuttleworth, a famous nineteenth-century reformer, represented the working-class home as "a space lacking certain boundaries."[3] Lockwood's confusion about the inhabitants displays middle-class fear of "the heaping and intermixing of bodies" (*NA,* 171).

Even the "penetralium" of the Heights, the grotesque carvings above the door, are significant of what is within: "a wilderness of crumbling griffins and shameless little boys" (46). The grotesque, say Stallybrass and White, is

> a boundary phenomenon of hybridization or inmixing, in which self and other become enmeshed in an inclusive, heterogeneous, danger-ously unstable zone. (*S&W*, 193)

Lockwood's confusion at the Heights is primarily manifested as an inability to sort out the family relationships: he cannot decide to whom the "fairy" (56) or "witch" (57) Cathy is married (55–56), whether the "clown" (55) Hareton is servant or heir (53–54), and whether Heathcliff is a "gypsy" or a "gentleman" (47). Patricia Yaeger points out that Lockwood commits an "amazing number of bloopers" in this scene.[4] His errors all involve an inability to determine social identities (suggesting that he is plunged into babyhood, before such relations are clear). He even mistakes a heap of dead rabbits for Cathy's kittens, being unable to distinguish pets from food or the dead from the living (52). Indeed, all the "pets" at the Heights exhibit the presence of violence. Lisa Surridge has pointed out that dogs fre-quently represent women in Victorian fiction, as a device for indi-rectly revealing domestic abuse (*LS*, 3). Lockwood recognizes but dis-misses the presence of domestic violence at the Heights: he had "no desire to be entertained by a cat and dog combat," he says of incipient "hostilities" between Cathy and Heathcliff (72). When Lockwood is himself attacked by the dogs, he compares them to "a herd of pos-sessed swine," (49) recalling the Bible story (Mark 5: 9–13) in which "unclean spirits are literally displaced from man to pigs" (*S&W*, 50). Inside the Heights animals represent people and people act like animals: Lockwood is clearly in a boundary zone where identity is unstable.

Lockwood's agitation at the Heights, and his obsession with get-ting into it, is redolent of sexual desire. His second attempt at entry, which he twice calls a "repetition of my intrusion" (50, 70), is prompted by the "spectacle" of a "servant-girl on her knees" (51) at the hearth of his own home. Stallybrass and White point out that a woman kneeling on all fours "was one of the habitual postures of the maid of all work," making her seem sexually accessible (*S&W*, 154). Recoiling in horror from this provocative sight, Lockwood dashes off to the Heights while "ejaculat[ing] mentally" (the text is careful to add "mentally"!) "I don't care—I *will* get in!" (51; my emphasis). But Lockwood is clearly very ambivalent about "getting in."

Lockwood's anxiety inside the Heights prompts him to recall his relationship with his mother and another woman about whom he was ambivalent. He recounts that while on holiday he had seen "a most fascinating creature, a real goddess in my eyes, as long as she took no notice of me," but as soon as she returned his looks, Lockwood "shrunk icily into myself, like a snail" (48). Beth Newman has observed that what Lockwood fears is the return of his gaze: when the woman looks back she threatens his control, his need to turn her into an object (*BN*, 1031). His reaction to Cathy is remarkably similar. So long as Cathy is a "beneficent fairy" (55) or a "little witch" (57), Lockwood does not have to confront her as a real woman. So long as he can gaze voyeuristically, he can offer a detailed description of her "whole figure and countenance." He comments that her eyes "would have been irresistible," except that "fortunately for my susceptible heart, the only sentiment they evinced hovered between scorn and a kind of desperation" (53). But perhaps it is because Cathy looks back that Lockwood finds her "unnatural" (53): "she kept her eyes on me, in a cool, regardless manner, exceedingly embarrassing and disagreeable" (52). Newman argues that the incident with the "goddess" at the seaside, which encapsulates Lockwood's attitudes towards women, is parodied by his attempt at the Heights to pet the "canine mother": "My caress provoked a long, guttural gnarl" (48), followed by an attack in which Lockwood tries to defend himself with a poker (an appropriate masculine symbol) (49). Newman argues convincingly that

> Lockwood fears . . . that his "real goddess" might have proved a
> bitch goddess, reciprocating his attentions as the four-footed bitch at
> the Heights does—with the threat of bodily mutilation. (*BN*, 1031)

Lockwood's fear, therefore, is the fear of castration, of losing his masculine power and control. Perhaps his intense embarrassment and his susceptibility to ridicule at the Heights arise from what his fear of the dogs really represents.

Lockwood's desire to enter the Heights is finally cured by the terrifying encounter at the heart of it. In place of another attempt to explore the house, Lockwood attempts to penetrate Nelly's story, declaring (with as much determination as "I will get in!") that he will "extract wholesome medicines from Mrs. Dean's bitter herbs" (191). Lockwood becomes a reader of Nelly's story, but the story is clearly interesting to him as a surrogate for the woman who has prompted his interest:

> Hearing a story about the object of his desire becomes a means of satisfying his desire to gaze at her, becomes a substitute, a metaphor, for the pleasure of looking. (*BN*, 1033)

Lockwood thus presents himself as a reader: his diary is a critical and interpretive effort to penetrate the mystery of the Heights. Furthermore, the penetration is a sublimation of a sexual desire: without wanting to be too blunt, we can see that Lockwood's penetration of Nelly's story relieves his fear of penetrating the woman's body.

Lockwood's famous nightmares combine anxiety about sex, particularly about sexual inadequacy and fear of femininity, with anxiety about texts. It seems that Lockwood's inability to interpret what he finds at the Heights issues in dreams of impotence. It is, as Carol Jacobs has argued, at least three texts which are the immediate cause of Lockwood's dreams: the names on the windowsill, Catherine's tomes, and Catherine's diary.[5] The scene in which Lockwood reads Catherine's diary is charged with sexual desire. Finding himself in Catherine's bed-chamber, Lockwood closes himself in the innermost closet. The window ledge is covered with inscriptions: *"Catherine Earnshaw . . . Catherine Heathcliff . . . Catherine Linton"* (61). When Lockwood tries to sleep the letters materialize into "spectres—the air swarmed with Catherines" (61). When he rather guiltily "spread[s] open" the diary on his knees, the "injured tome" seems to be Catherine herself (62). The odor of roasted skin which makes Lockwood feel sick—from the hot candle "reclining" on the volume—suggests a human victim, especially when we remember that for the Victorians, as Davidoff puts it, "female sexuality was directly associated with uncleanness and especially odour" (*LD*, 137 n. 32). I wonder whether the reclining candle suggests that it is Lockwood's impotence as a reader which injures Catherine's diary? Certainly the distinction between Catherine and "her book" is blurred when Lockwood begins to "decypher her faded hieroglyphics" (62), the same terms used by Freud for reading the symptoms of hysteria in his patients.[6] Woman, for Freud, remained an insoluble mystery, and it seems that Catherine is equally enigmatic. Lockwood reads very little of her diary; *Wuthering Heights* later hints, we shall see, that he has also been masturbating, and he soon falls asleep.

Lockwood's dreams reveal fear of sexuality and of textuality. In the first dream he is being guided by Joseph over a white space, reminiscent of the margins of a page, to his home, but is told that he will "never get into the house" without a "heavy-headed cudgel" such as the one which Joseph is "boastfully flourishing" (65). Entry into the house, which apparently requires a phallus, is immediately substituted by entry into a text: "Then, a new idea flashed across me. I was not going there; we were journeying to hear the famous Jabes Branderham preach from the text" (65). The landscape of this dream is a sinister female anatomy: "a hollow, between two hills—an elevated hollow—near a swamp, whose peaty moisture is said to answer all the purposes of embalming on the few corpses deposited there" (65). Like D.G. Rossetti's *The Orchard Pit*, this "dream-scape" exhibits dread of female sexuality.[7] Lockwood's distress about the sermon to which he is subjected results, as Jacobs has pointed out, not from its contents but from its very textuality: "The length of the text and especially the repetitive nature of its structure make its textuality more prevalent than its content" (*CJ*, 52). But it is the text's impenetrability which Lockwood fears: "it is ultimately the endless text which wields the power to destroy Lockwood" (*CJ*, 53). His attempt to object to the sermon results in the "whole assembly" rushing round him "in a body," all "exalting their pilgrim's staves," to "execute upon him the judgement written" (66). As Jacobs says, Lockwood is assaulted by the text; I would add that he is also castrated, physically marked as lacking what the others have, the (aggressive) phallus. Lockwood's first dream, then, combines fear of sexuality with anxiety about textuality. Without the phallic staff he can enter neither the space of home nor the space of the text (of Branderham's sermon). The dream text is embodied in a feminine landscape which is fatally threatening. Lockwood fears castration by a feminine text.

The next dream is a personification of the name "Catherine Linton" on the windowsill, although it is significant that it personifies itself (the term is Lockwood's) as a ghost (69). Lockwood hears an insistent tapping at the window which annoys him so much that although the casement is soldered shut he attempts to silence it by putting his fist "through the glass, and stretching an arm out to seize the importunate branch: instead of which, my fingers closed on the fingers of a little, ice-cold hand!" (67). The "intense horror" of the tenacious grip makes him "cruel," and

> finding it useless to attempt shaking the creature off, I pulled its wrist onto the broken pane, and rubbed it to and fro till the blood ran down and soaked the bedclothes: still it wailed, "Let me in!" and maintained its tenacious gripe, almost maddening me with fear.
> "How can I!" I said at length. "Let *me* go, if you want me to let you in!"
> The fingers relaxed, I snatched mine through the hole, hurriedly piled the books up in a pyramid against it, and stopped my ears to exclude the lamentable prayer. (67)

This, one of the most frequently discussed passages in English literature, is often regarded as sexual in nature: Lockwood, in Catherine's bed, sheds her blood on the bedclothes after breaking through a fragile membrane.[8] It is also a classic example of male fear of sexual intercourse: Lockwood is held in a tenacious grip, and is so afraid that he becomes violent. Musselwhite argues that the dream represents Lockwood's confrontation with the terrible "Other," the price he pays for reading between the lines of the tomes, or, in other words, for penetrating the text (*DM*, 156). Luce Irigaray would remind us that woman represents "a *hole* in men's signifying economy."[9] Catherine is found in the gaps of the patriarchal tomes, she personifies into a ghost, a specter. Yet Lockwood is terrified by this spectacle of feminine sexuality. "Why," asks Irigaray, "this fear, horror, phobia, . . . [sic] felt when there is nothing to be seen? Why does having nothing that can be seen threaten his libidinal economy?" Could it be fear that "the 'nothing to be seen' . . . might yet have some reality"? (*SW*, 49, 50). Lockwood's dream manifests his fear of the spectacle of the female genitals, which are figured as a "gap" or a "hole" in phallocentric theories such as Freud's (*SW*, 50). Irigaray argues that men's fear of feminine sexuality results from their repressed knowledge that there is "something to be seen" in the gap. "Woman's sexuality," comments Irigaray, "is no doubt the most basic form of the *unheimlich*" (*SW*, 47–48 n. 29). This is especially appropriate to Lockwood's fear of the ghost, since the *unheimlich,* or uncanny, is, according to Freud, a projection of repressed knowledge. Lockwood's fear of femininity is directly linked in his dreams to his fear of the text: his attempt at penetration leads to this horrifying spectacle of the "hole."

When Lockwood screams and Heathcliff rushes in demanding an explanation, Lockwood doesn't admit to having looked into the testaments because he feels guilty and embarrassed about "knowledge of their written, as well as their printed contents" (69). Instead he says he was "spelling over the name scratched on that window-ledge. A monotonous occupation, calculated to set me asleep, like counting, or—" (69). Musselwhite has commented that the hyphen here "is perhaps not innocent" (*DM*, 156), meaning that Lockwood was masturbating. The likelihood that Lockwood was doing something which could not be told is further supported by Charlotte Brontë's remarks in the Preface that her sister didn't use hyphens to replace offensive words: "I cannot tell," she says, "what feeling it spares—what horror it conceals" (38). In other words, Emily Brontë believed that the practice of blanks is hypocritical since we all know what is there anyway. Her use of a hyphen in this case is thus doubly significant. Masturbation was so taboo in the nineteenth century that it was unmentionable: one respected medical authority on the subject wrote about it only in Latin for fear that he would be accused of titillation.[10] Furthermore,

Lockwood's guilt at his occupation is manifested in the dream he has on falling asleep, in which he accuses Jabes Branderham of "the sin that no Christian need pardon" (66). The unpardonable "sin" is very likely that which the Victorians called "onanism" or self-love. Their phobia was due to the asocial nature of masturbation: if sexual pleasure could be obtained outside of the procreative couple, then this undermined what was assumed to be a "natural" social order.

Emily Brontë must have known how any reader would react to the elision in the text, and Heathcliff's outrage seems to confirm it: "'What *can* you mean by talking in this way to *me?*' thundered Heathcliff with savage vehemence. 'How *dare* you, under my roof?' . . ." (69). Heathcliff reacts as though Lockwood has indeed stolen his lover. To mollify Heathcliff, Lockwood explains that his dreams were a personification of Catherine's names: "affirming I had never heard the appellation of 'Catherine Linton,' before, but reading it often over produced an impression which personified itself when I had no longer my imagination under control" (69). Lockwood admits to losing control of his imagination; nothing could speak more clearly, to the Victorians, of the nature of Lockwood's reading. There was thought to be a dangerous connection between reverie and "self-pollution," so that young men were warned to avoid certain kinds of reading: "In connection with these books, allow me to lift up a loud voice against those rovings of the imagination, by which the mind is at once enfeebled, and the heart and feelings debased and polluted" (quoted in *BB*, 173). It isn't clear whether this author blames the books themselves, or the way they are read, for prompting the sin of masturbation. Although, as we shall see, the implication that Lockwood was masturbating is an important clue to the nature of Catherine's diary and of *Wuthering Heights* itself, it also reveals a great deal about Lockwood's reading habits. Lockwood's furtive and self-confessedly guilty reading of Catherine's diary gives him sexual gratification: his invasion of her private thoughts is a sublimation of invasion of her body. Lockwood's attitude to women, we have seen, reduces them to something else—a goddess, a fairy, a witch—which serves to confirm his masculinity and to shore up his power (we've seen that he rejects those women who look back at him). But when Lockwood attempts to penetrate the

Heights in search of the enigma of Cathy, he finds himself lacking in his customary power and control: he is confused, weak, disoriented, foolish. When Joseph calls Cathy a "nowt"—of no consequence— Lockwood assumes that the insult was directed at himself: "Bud yah're a nowt, and it's noa use talking—yah'll niver mend uh yer ill ways; bud, goa raight tuh t' divil, like yer mother afore ye!" (57). The "nowt" or zero is also a metaphor, we've seen, for femininity. In the Heights Lockwood is placed in a feminine position, and he dreams of being deprived of the phallus, of being castrated.

From being an "insider," Lockwood becomes an outsider; he is rendered marginal and vulnerable at the Heights and in his dreams. In the first dream he is to be publicly excommunicated for an unknown and unwitting sin. He is accused in the Chapel of "odd transgressions that I never imagined previously" (65). Like women in the eyes of the Church—who inherit the sins of Eve, and like their "mother afore ye" will go "raight tuh t' divil"—Lockwood is simply guilty.

Lockwood's masturbatory dreams in response to Catherine's diary confirm that it had taken a powerful hold of him, just as *Wuthering Heights* itself had affected one early reviewer: "when we lay aside the book it is some time before we can persuade ourselves that we have held nothing more than imaginary intercourse with the ideal creations of the brain" (*CH,* 231). Reading Catherine's diary leads Lockwood into "intercourse" with "an ideal creature." The books that the Victorians feared would lead to "self-pollution" were those in which excessive passion might cause unhealthy wanderings of the imagination. It is clear that Catherine's diary has an adverse effect on Lockwood's imagination: the fact that he masturbates over it reveals the subversive nature of the diary, and, we shall see, of *Wuthering Heights* itself.

CATHERINE'S DIARY

Catherine's diary is the "key" which unlocks the narrative of the Heights, for both Lockwood and the reader. The quotation marks surrounding the extract from the diary in the text of *Wuthering Heights* indicate that Lockwood is quoting directly, in which case this is the only time that Catherine tells her own story. As we've seen, Lockwood discovers Catherine's diary in the margins of an old "tome":

> Catherine's library was select; and its state of dilapidation proved it to have been well used, though not altogether for a legitimate purpose; scarcely one chapter had escaped a pen and ink commentary— at least the appearance of one—covering every morsel of blank that the printer had left. (62)

On the one hand, Catherine's choice of the margins for her autobiography can be seen to represent her marginal social status as a woman, but on the other, it can be seen as rebellion against that position. Anyone who has ever defaced a sacred text will appreciate the subversive nature of Catherine's marginalia (further emphasized, as we saw in the last chapter, by Lockwood's masturbating over it). Catherine uses the margins of "Testaments" to describe throwing such books into the dog kennel, and ripping them apart; writing all over them, however, seems a much more effective protest. Catherine's diary, as we noted in the introduction, employs the very strategies advocated by the French feminist Luce Irigaray to undermine the dominant patriarchal discourses of Western culture. Irigaray maintains that women need to interrogate male texts by filling in the gaps, by attending to what is repressed for the sake of coherence "in order to pry out of them what they have borrowed that is feminine, from the feminine, to make them 'render up' and give back what they owe the feminine" (*TS,* 74). Catherine's diary, which fills "every morsel of blank" in the sacred texts, is regarded by Lockwood as an illegitimate reading, but for Irigaray it would constitute "a process of interpretive rereading" (*TS,* 75). It could be argued that to write only in the margins is to confirm one's oppressed status, but it also represents what Irigaray calls an "excess on the feminine side": Catherine goes beyond, rises above, the values of her society, an excess which is enacted by her writing (*TS,* 78).

What first attracts Lockwood to Catherine's diary is "an excellent caricature of my friend Joseph, rudely yet powerfully sketched" (62). Parody is another strategy advocated and practiced by Irigaray in order to "challenge, and *disrupt*" patriarchal discourse (*TS*, 74). It is Joseph, we learn from the diary, who administers the teachings of the "good books": he subjects the children to a three-hour "homily for his own sake" (62). It is Joseph, as we shall see, who occupies the central place at the Heights, and in the novel, as upholder of the status quo. The values which he represents, and against which Catherine and Heathcliff rebel, are contained in the books which the children attempt to destroy and deface. Nelly Dean, who also voices conventional values and pieties, explicitly connects moral transgression to exclusion from the teachings of the "good books": she accuses both Catherine and Heathcliff, at different times, of ignoring or going beyond the precepts of the Bible (122, 363).

Joseph, we are told, "ransacks" the Bible in order to "fling the curses on his neighbours" (83). Thus he reads both violently, and—like Lockwood reading Catherine's diary for sexual titillation—in a way which violates the text; it also reveals the interrelationship between treatment of texts and treatment of others in *Wuthering Heights:* Joseph "flings" curses at his neighbors. Joseph's choice curses are directed at women: we have already seen him calling Cathy a "nowt." Catherine's diary, written in the margins, represents a different, more appropriately "feminine," approach to texts: rather than penetrating (like Lockwood), or dismembering (like Joseph), Catherine engulfs the text with her own writing. Catherine's diary, as we saw from Lockwood's nightmares, is the very kind of endless and open text that he fears. Furthermore, in Irigaray's view, Catherine retrieves the repressed feminine in the tomes, showing that there is something to be reckoned with in the gap of phallocentric discourse.

Catherine's diary throws a great deal of light on *Wuthering Heights* itself because in many respects it is a microcosm of the novel. Identifying disobedience as originating in injustice and maltreatment, both are records of rebellion against the constrictions of social convention and family oppression. Stylistically, both employ irony and satire to gain the reader's attention. Lockwood's interest in the diary is "kindled" by the caricature of Joseph, just as the reader's interest is kindled by the satirical portrait of Lockwood in the opening pages of the novel. Finally, both can be seen as marginal works: Catherine's to the Testaments and Bronte's (if we are to believe F. R. Leavis) to the "Great Tradition" of the English literary canon.[11] In style as well as content, Catherine's diary bears a striking resemblance to *Wuthering Heights* itself. Although critics frequently present Lockwood as the surrogate reader in the text, Catherine as a reader and commentator of texts is always overlooked; yet what her diary offers us is an alternative reading and writing strategy—what Roland Barthes would call a "writerly" reading of the "good books"—one which enables her to assert herself in relation to them.[12]

Like *Wuthering Heights,* the diary employs spatial metaphor to express social or familial status. While the "paradise on the hearth" (63) is occupied by Hindley and his wife, Catherine and Heathcliff are literally banished to the peripheries: "a mere titter is sufficient to send us into corners!" (63). While "Hindley and his wife basked down stairs before a comfortable fire, doing anything but reading their Bibles" (62), Catherine, Heathcliff and the plough-boy are "commanded to take our Prayer-books and mount" to the garret, to be confined for three hours "groaning and shivering," listening to Joseph's sermon. The children then attempt to create a little haven—"we made ourselves as snug as our means allowed in the arch of the dresser" (63)—by fastening their pinafores to make a curtain. But, like the "closet" in which Lockwood reads Catherine's diary, the apparent sanctuary is violently intruded upon: "in comes Joseph, on an errand from the stables. He tears down my handywork, boxes my ears, and croaks" that with their father just buried the children should not be "laiking" (or larking) but rather reading "good books" and thinking "uh yer sowls!" (63). The struggle between the generations is violent—the children are frequently hit—and revolves around the "good books" which are forced on the younger ones while Hindley and Frances are free to ignore theirs.

Not surprisingly, the children direct their resentment at the "lumber" that is "thrust" on them: "I took my dingy volume by the scroop, and hurled it into the dog-kennel, vowing I hated a good book" (63). When the children are in turn "hurled" into the "back-kitchen" to await the advent of the devil they seem very vulnerable (63). Catherine seeks solace by writing in her diary, but Heathcliff prefers a different marginal space, and he persuades Catherine to seek freedom on the moors:

> I reached this book, and a pot of ink from the shelf, and pushed the house-door ajar to give me light, and I have got the time on with writing for twenty minutes; but my companion is impatient and proposes that we should appropriate the dairy woman's cloak, and have a scamper on the moors, under its shelter . . .—we cannot be damper, or colder, in the rain that we are here. (64)

Catherine's diary uses location to dramatize social hierarchy: Hindley, the legal heir to the house, occupies the hearth, while Catherine and Heathcliff are banished to the corners, under tables, the garret, the back-kitchen, and the moors. Hindley wants to expel Heathcliff entirely:

> Poor Heathcliff! Hindley calls him a vagabond, and won't let him sit with us, nor eat with us any more; and, he says, he and I must not play together, and threatens to turn him out of the house if we break his orders. (64)

Catherine and Heathcliff react to their enforced marginalization by making a private virtue of necessity: they wholly reject the "good books" that are forced on them, and instead inhabit marginal spaces of their own creating: Catherine chooses her diary while Heathcliff prefers the moors (64). Catherine's diary is the literary equivalent of the moors: both offer liberation from oppressive values and ideologies.

Lockwood's reaction to marginalization is very different. As we have seen, he is terrified of the space that Catherine seeks to inhabit through her diary. The day after he reads the diary and sees the specter at the heart of it, Lockwood's disorientation is expressed through his dismay at finding all familiar signposts to home obliterated: his nightmare has become a reality. Two lengthy paragraphs (which are, we should remember, Lockwood's diary) are devoted to describing how the snow had filled up treacherous pits, and the signs to warn of "deep swamps on either hand" of "the firmer path" had "vanished"

WUTHERING HEIGHTS

(73). The symbolism is clear: Lockwood is terrified of straying from the known path, the conventional values and phallocentrism inherited from his society. Catherine and Heathcliff, on the other hand, find the same values oppressive and constrictive, so that they seek marginalization, though as we shall see, in very different ways.

6

The Values at the Center:
Joseph and Nelly

We have seen so far that *Wuthering Heights* employs spatial metaphors in two interrelated ways: the habitually preferred location of characters indicates a great deal about their social and emotional lives; their social relationships are in turn reflected in their attitudes to texts. We have seen Lockwood invading Catherine's bed and her diary. The following chapters elaborate on the link in *Wuthering Heights* between the vulnerability of spaces and the vulnerability of women, and how the men's need to protect their own space or to invade others' spaces expresses their desire to protect masculine dominance.

Furthermore, the characters' varying responses to others is linked to their attitudes towards books and texts. The connection may not at first seem obvious, but it is clear, for example, that Lockwood and Catherine have very different approaches to texts, which are inseparable from their attitudes towards themselves and others. Catherine's diary covers the blank spaces of texts with her own story of rebellion; Lockwood produces *his* diary by prying into, and taking off from, Catherine's.

In this chapter we shall explore the ways in which Joseph and Nelly represent and voice the dominant values of Victorian bourgeois society, providing the central point from which Heathcliff and Catherine can be seen as deviant. The rebellion of Heathcliff and Catherine, their deliberate self-marginalization, is justified by the unattractive values embodied in Joseph and Nelly Dean.

JOSEPH

Joseph is an extremely important character in *Wuthering Heights,* who aptly demonstrates the significance of location, and the link between treatment of texts and of others. Joseph, the manservant at the Heights, has been almost entirely ignored by critics, and yet he is of central significance, both literally and symbolically: he inhabits the center of the Heights and embodies the mainstream values of his society, against which are pitted Catherine, Heathcliff (to a lesser extent), and *Wuthering Heights* itself.

Van de Laar points out that Joseph's location at the Heights signifies his role: "Joseph's window is at the top of the house, overlooking the Heights. Thus Joseph is connected with the heart of the story" (*VL,* 94). But *how* is Joseph connected with the heart of the story? He is usually pictured near the fire (178, 269, 282, 342, 348, 366), traditionally the center of family life. Joseph considers it his "awn heathstun" (348), and his private heaven (just as Catherine, Cathy, Linton, and Heathcliff all describe theirs [121, 280, 363]):

> Joseph seemed sitting in a sort of elysium alone, beside a roaring fire; a quart of ale on the table near him, bristling with large pieces of toasted oat cake; and his black, short pipe in his mouth. (269)

But the conventional image of domestic bliss is here reversed. Joseph's closeness to the fire associates him with the devil: "I heard a malignant, crackly laugh by the fire, and turning beheld that odious Joseph, standing rubbing his bony hands, and quivering" (282). His expression of glee is evoked by Hareton's violence towards Cathy and Linton.

The Values at the Center: Joseph and Nelly

If Joseph were not somewhat deflated by the text's satirical treatment of him, he would be strongly reminiscent of Iago in William Shakespeare's *Othello*. He is hypocritical, self-righteous, domineering, superior, and judgmental; fortunately his attempts to manipulate others only occasionally succeed. Early in the narrative Joseph appropriates the role of the father: "the more feeble the master became, the more influence he gained" (83). Even when Earnshaw senior is dying, Joseph is "relentless in worrying him about his soul's concerns, and about ruling his children rigidly" (83). Each "master" of the Heights—Earnshaw, Hindley, Heathcliff—is urged by Joseph to greater severity and harshness; he is the self-appointed conscience, a kind of external super-ego, of the other characters.

As well as being situated at the center of the Heights, Joseph has a "preference for locked doors and gates" (*VL*, 123): he tries to impose the restrictions of his conventional values on others. Through Joseph, says Felicia Gordon, Brontë "mocks some of the worst aspects of Calvinism: a spiteful, self-righteous fanaticism."[1] But, "to be fair," she claims, he does attempt to correct the "dramatic excesses of the other characters. In an odd way, Joseph does represent moral stability." While it is true that Joseph represents stability—he is the only character in the novel who goes nowhere, either literally or symbolically—his conservatism is so oppressive that it provokes rebellion: "his peevish reproofs awakened in [Catherine] a naughty delight to provoke him" (83). No wonder Joseph's example prompts Catherine to "vow" she "hated a good book" (63).

Joseph's aspirations to tyranny are associated throughout the novel with religious texts, especially the Bible. His harsh, even damning, criticisms of others usually take the form of an invocation of religious writings (57, 63, 126, 339) to which he is "fanatically addicted" (*VL*, 200). He can quote at length, even giving the citations, from the Bible (125–26). Nelly introduces Joseph into the narrative as "the wearisomest, self-righteous pharisee that ever ransacked a Bible to rake the promises to himself, and fling the curses on his neighbours" (82–83). By using religious texts as instruments of oppression, Joseph does violence to the text and to others: he "ransacks" the Bible and "flings" its curses at people.

Joseph also, in one of the most shocking scenes in the novel, uses his Bible to hoard money. "Deeply" affected by the sight of Cathy "stealing" Hareton from him, and "his emotion . . . only revealed by the immense sighs he drew," Joseph

> solemnly spread his large Bible on the table, and overlaid it with dirty bank-notes from his pocket-book, the produce of the day's transactions. (346)

Joseph therefore consoles himself for the loss of his "lad" (339) with what is popularly known as filthy lucre: the dirtiness of the money underlines his hypocrisy in using the Bible in a manner utterly contradictory to its teachings. Furthermore, Joseph's spreading open of the Bible echoes Lockwood spreading open Catherine's diary: both men use, or misuse, texts similarly. Both men adopt aggressive, if not violent, reading strategies, which in *Wuthering Heights* are almost exclusively masculine (Nelly is an exception), and which accompany similar attitudes to women.

Joseph is the most blatantly misogynist character in the novel. His calling Cathy a "nowt" would perhaps be relatively insignificant were it not reinforced and elaborated by other remarks he makes about and to the women. The worst fate that Joseph can imagine for Heathcliff when he is missing is to be at the bottom of a "bog-hoile," which further connects him to Lockwood's dream, with its fear of a landscape representing femininity. Joseph frequently refers to women as "hoiles" (holes) in some form. When he sees Cathy caressing Hareton, Joseph makes a bid for him by remarking: "This hoile's norther mensful, nor seemly fur us—we mun side aht, and seearch another!" (346). The proposal to slide out of an unseemly hole conveys Joseph's disgust at what he perceives to be Cathy's seduction of Hareton: "It's yon flaysome, graceless quean, ut's witched ahr lad, wi' her bold een, un' her forrard ways—till—Nay! it fair brusts my heart! . . ." (349). Cathy has, Joseph believes, stolen Hareton's very "soul" with her looks and her bold eye. Like the "fascinating creature" (48) whom Lockwood watched at the seaside, Cathy poses a threat to Joseph because she dares to look back. Like Lockwood, Joseph regards women as spectacles for male contemplation: he wishes to reduce them to "nowts"—to objects— because their femininity frightens him. He trembles "with sincere horror" when Cathy teases him by saying she is learning the "Black Art" in order to cast a spell on him (57).

Joseph does not see Nelly as a threat, because, he says, she's not sufficiently physically attractive: "Nasty, ill nowt as shoo is, Thank God! *shoo* cannot stale t'sowl uh nob'dy! Shoo wer niver so handsome, bud whet a body mud look at her 'baht winking" (349). Cathy, on the other hand, threatens Joseph so severely that (as we shall see in chapter 10) he is described as "unmanned" by her (349). He feels that her "witching" of Hareton has desecrated his Bible: "Aw cannut oppen t'Blessed Book, bud yah set up them glories tuh sattan, un'all t'flaysome wickednesses ut iver wer born intuh t'warld!" (339). The threat posed by Cathy to Joseph's manhood takes the form of her incursions into his jealously protected domains—his books and his garden. Imprisoned at the Heights, Cathy secretly reads Joseph's books, smuggles in her own (341), and then brings her plants from the Grange to create her own flower garden in the midst of Joseph's fruit trees (347). This flower bed—which as we shall see (chap. 10) is strongly reminiscent of her mother's marginal space in the "good books"—is what finally "unmans" Joseph:

> Aw mun hev my wage, and Aw mun goa! Aw *hed* aimed tuh dee, wheare Aw'd sarved fur sixty years; un' Aw thowt Aw'd lug my books up intuh t'garret, 'un all my bits uh stuff, un' they sud hev t'kitchen tuh theirseln; fur t'sake uh quietness. It wur hard tuh gie up my awn heathstun, bud Aw thowt Aw *could* do that! Bud, nah, shoo's taan my garden frough me, un' by th' heart! Maister, Aw cannot stand it! (348).

Joseph is "unmanned by a sense of his bitter injuries": without his land he is without his masculinity. Although Irigaray is being somewhat humorous when she describes Western discourse as dominated by the male values of "property, production, order, form, unity, visibility . . . and erection" (*TS*, 86), it is a surprisingly accurate assessment of Joseph's fetishes: he values property and erection, and what they represent—capital and masculinity—as though the two were interdependent. In Lockwood's dream, it is Joseph who boastfully flourishes the phallic cudgel as the only sign of access to the Grange and the Chapel, those bastions of conservative and patriarchal values.

NELLY DEAN

Joseph's location at the center of the Heights and his use of the Bible to coerce others signify his role as upholder of a repressive and sexist status quo. Nelly Dean's predilection for particular locations similarly indicates her function as another guardian of conservative and patriar-chal values, but Nelly's position is more complex than Joseph's. Nelly is overwhelmingly associated with borders—windows, doors, gates, walls; although her function as housemaid makes her in some respects socially peripheral, she occupies a central role in the novel as nar-rator and, ironically, as guardian of the very limits of middle-class respectability which marginalize her.

Van de Laar sees the "remarkable number" of images of bound-aries associated with Nelly as symbolizing "the idea of penetration":

> Taken together doors, windows, gates, keys, walls, mirrors and por-traits, occurring in as many as 65 passages with relation to Nelly, cannot but reflect strongly her wish to know everything that is going on about her, to penetrate into everybody's secret thoughts and feel-ings. She is frequently seen listening at doors, opening windows to see and hear, rattling the handles of locked doors. (*VL*, 112)

Although Nelly's frequent proximity to doors and windows enables her to function as the narrator of the story, the action takes place before the telling of it, so that it doesn't account for the extent of her curiosity. Kavanagh finds it puzzling that Nelly's narrative voice is so often regarded as providing an objective "common sense" view of events, because she is so clearly actively "interested" in what happens. Certainly she alters events. Kavanagh is right that Nelly hides "her own active role in defending certain imaginary values and advancing certain imaginary interests" (*JK*, 34).

Even when she appears to be merely a passive observer, Nelly can be seen to be "advancing certain . . . interests." Gilbert and Gubar argue that Nelly "manages to avoid taking sides—or, rather, like a wall, she is related to both sides" (*G&G*, 290). A wall, however, can divide people, can contribute to conflict. The most decisive scene in the novel, which many critics argue is the point at which Catherine's choice makes the future tragedy, is that in which Catherine declares— overheard by Heathcliff—that it would degrade her to marry him. Yet it is Nelly who allows Heathcliff to hear what he does: she neither interrupts Catherine nor tries to prevent Heathcliff from leaving before Catherine has explained how much she loves him:

> Ere this speech ended, I became sensible of Heathcliff's presence. Having noticed a slight movement, I turned my head, and saw him rise from the bench, and steal out, noiselessly. He had listened till he heard Catherine say it would degrade her to marry him, and then he stayed to hear no farther. (121)

At another decisive moment Nelly speaks aloud in order to draw Catherine's attention to Heathcliff kissing Isabella in the garden: " 'Judas! Traitor!' I ejaculated. 'You are a hypocrite, too, are you? a deliberate deceiver?' " (150). Nelly's interference can be yet more destructive. When she discovers Cathy's letters from Linton, she burns them, and then tells Edgar about the relationship soon after promising Cathy that she wouldn't (260–61, 286). Nelly too can be a "Judas," it seems.

Just before her death, Catherine calls Nelly a "traitor" and a "hidden enemy" (166). Nelly's hypocrisy is almost as obvious as Joseph's, and she certainly has more influence than he does. She often advises her masters and admonishes her mistresses. Unlike Joseph's, Nelly's advice is usually heeded. She tells Edgar, for example, that it is time to have Heathcliff's visits on a different footing, and that he should not be so "soft" with his wife about it (152). We shall see that Edgar's and Heathcliff's subsequent conflict leads directly to Catherine's death.

Nelly's actions, as "general mother," make her, as many critics have pointed out, "patriarchy's paradigmatic housekeeper," "charged with the task of policing the realm" (*G&G*, 291, 295; *JK*, 32; *LP*,

102). What is less frequently remarked is that Nelly defends "patriarchal, or more precisely . . . gentry values" (*LP*, 102), by struggling to keep others "in line" physically as well as morally. Nelly guards borders, attempting to keep people inside them. It is Nelly who ensures that Cathy does not wander beyond the walls of Thrushcross Grange—"The grange is not a prison, Ellen, and you are not my jailer" (275), says Cathy, having escaped through a broken gate. Similarly, it is Nelly who struggles to keep Catherine from opening the window onto the moors just before her death. Because Nelly refuses to open the window, "Catherine . . . realizes the hidden enmity in" her (*VL*, 116). Nelly's struggle with Heathcliff just before he dies is also "reflected in the opening and shutting of doors and windows" (*VL*, 122). Both Catherine and Heathcliff strain for the freedom of the moors at the end of their lives, while Nelly exerts herself to keep them indoors (163, 357, 359); the struggle for souls is waged over the opening and closing of windows. In this sense, Gilbert and Gubar are right that Nelly is a kind of wall: one which protects "respectability."

Although Nelly attempts to confine men and women to conventional behavior, her harshest criticisms, like Joseph's, are directed at the women, whose stepping out of line she regards as a failure of feminine "duty." When Catherine proposes to marry Edgar although she loves Heathcliff, Nelly invokes Christian teachings by calling her a "wicked unprincipled girl," who is ignorant of the "duties you undertake in marrying" (122). When Isabella similarly defies the marriage vows, Nelly scolds "Fie, fie, Miss! . . . One might suppose you had never opened a Bible in your life" (215). Heathcliff also is reminded by Nelly, just before he dies, that he "hardly had a Bible in your hands" in his whole life, and that he had erred "very far" from "its precepts" (363). Nelly, then, sees personal rebellion as rejection of the Bible. Like Joseph, Nelly thoughtlessly inflicts the Bible on others, exhorting them to remain within its precepts.

Nelly's conventional piety is, like Joseph's, exposed and implicitly criticized in the novel. After Catherine's death, Nelly says that "I am seldom otherwise than happy while watching in the chamber of death . . . I see a repose that neither earth nor hell can break" (201–2). Yet the reader knows full well that Catherine is *not* in repose: we have seen her desperate ghost, at the beginning of the novel, begging to be let in to the Heights (67).

Nelly calls herself a "cool spectator" (195) of Catherine's illness; she regards it as a manifestation of Catherine's willfulness, her failure to observe her "duties": "I could not get rid of the notion that she acted a part of her disorder" (159). Because Isabella runs away from Heathcliff when she is pregnant, Nelly is scandalized: "Laughter is sadly out of place under this roof, and in your condition!" (208). Although Isabella bears the marks of Heathcliff's brutality, Nelly seems to blame her for her appearance, telling her to be "more charitable" towards her husband. Nelly describes Isabella as though she were a fallen woman:

> She certainly seemed in no laughing predicament: her hair streaming on her shoulders, dripping with snow and water; she was dressed in the girlish dress she commonly wore, befitting her age more than her position; a low frock, with short sleeves, and nothing on either head or neck. The frock was of light silk, and clung to her with wet; and her feet were protected merely by thin slippers; add to this a deep cut under one ear, which only the cold prevented from bleeding profusely, a white face scratched and bruised, and a frame hardly able to support itself through fatigue, and you may fancy my first fright was not much allayed when I had leisure to examine her. (206–7)

Nelly clearly regards Isabella herself as responsible for her plight: her bodily abandon denotes personal laxity, a lack of respectable control. In a similar way, Catherine's "bold, saucy look" and loose tongue, as a child, were regarded by Nelly as indicating a propensity to looseness in other, more serious, ways (83–84). Nelly regards such female transgressions as a threat to social cohesion: she reminds Catherine and Isabella alike that they must observe their "duties" (122, 215). Nelly, as Gilbert and Gubar point out, is the "censorious agent of patriarchy" (*G&G*, 292). Nelly's use of the Bible resembles Joseph's: it "inspires" her "to some sharp-tongued criticisms and pretentious moral lessons" (*VL*, 198). Nelly, says Van de Laar, "is not free from a certain amount of self-righteousness and hypocrisy in her role of self-appointed moralist" (*VL*, 198).

Although Nelly admits to "little faith" in Catherine's principles "and still less sympathy for her feelings" (146), she reveals to Lockwood the most intimate details of her mistress's life. "Woman," says Irigaray, "is only a more or less obliging prop for the enactment of man's fantasies" (*TS*, 25); Nelly offers Catherine as an "obliging prop" for Lockwood's fantasies. Lockwood admires Nelly's story-telling, and thanks her for satisfying his voyeuristic needs, saying that he is in

> the mood of mind in which, if you were seated alone, and the cat licking its kitten on the rug before you, you would watch the operation so intently that puss's neglect of one ear would put you seriously out of temper. (102)

Lockwood flatters Nelly that she "has thought a great deal more than the generality of servants think" (103), and Nelly replies: "I have read more than you would fancy, Mr. Lockwood. You could not open a book in this library that I have not looked into, and got something out of also" (103). Nelly's reading is thus another manifestation of her intense curiosity: we can easily imagine her looking into, and "checking out," as we say now, every book in her master's library. Nelly's reading resembles Lockwood's prying into Catherine's journal and (thanks to Nelly) her private life. Nelly describes herself "looking into" and "getting something out of" her master's books, just as Lockwood is determined to "extract" something from Nelly's story. Nelly is alone among the female characters in displaying a "phallocentric" attitude to texts: she uses scripture to shame people into conformity, and she offers her story of Catherine for Lockwood's titillation.

Nelly's "internalisation of patriarchy's values" ironically polices the very boundaries that marginalize her. Lyn Pykett is sympathetic to Nelly's status as a "relative creature" in the two families, "biologically and legally related to no-one in the text," and yet "defined and determined by her position within a system of family relationships as daughter, sister, wife or mother" (*LP*, 104). Perhaps Nelly's "treachery," as Catherine sees it, results from occupying more than one position simultaneously: her maternal-sisterly relationship with each Catherine conflicts with her loyalty to Edgar, her brother-father.

The Values at the Center: Joseph and Nelly

Nelly's "relative" status makes her vulnerable to abuse as well as co-optation by the men. We shall see that the patriarchal society depicted in *Wuthering Heights* manifests violent appropriation of the women. If Nelly is more resigned, she also seems more resilient than any other female character, except perhaps Cathy. Perhaps it is her very conventionality which protects her: she has little trouble discerning, and deciding on, her "duties." Although Joseph, in his sexist way, claims that Nelly is not attractive enough to get a man to fall in love with her (349), there is nevertheless an erotic undercurrent to her relationship with Hindley, whose son Hareton is nursed by her. For the duration of Hindley's violent and self-destructive alcoholism, Nelly is in the position of an abused wife, trying to protect herself and Hareton from Hindley's outbursts. One of their many confrontations not only has clear sexual connotations, but attests to Nelly's extraordinary power of self-preservation:

> He held the knife in his hand, and pushed its point between my teeth: but, for my part, I was never much afraid of his vagaries. I spat it out, and affirmed it tasted detestably—I would not take it on any account. (114)

Perhaps the most telling image of Nelly's relationship with Hindley is her vision of him as a child at "a favourite spot twenty years ago." The vision turns out to be Hareton, who throws rocks and foul language at her; the child's violence and abuse is characteristic of the male characters in the novel, and helps to explain the significance of Nelly's vision:

> I gazed long at the weather-worn block; and, stooping down, perceived a hole near the bottom still full of snail-shells and pebbles, which we were very fond of storing there with more perishable things—and, as fresh as reality, it appeared that I beheld my early playmate seated on the withered turf, his dark, square head bent forward, and his little hand scooping out the earth with a piece of slate. (147)

The vision of the children's hole full of treasures bears a surprising resemblance to Catherine's death-bed vision (discussed in chap. 10) of

the lapwing's nest which she and Heathcliff discovered in their childhood: both are recollected visions evoking childhood emotions, of a
nest in the ground which once contained living things but now holds
only skeletons or empty shells (160). Nelly's vision is one of three
images in the novel of a plundered or despoiled nest, and all are associated with the major female characters, Nelly, Catherine, and Cathy.
Nelly's recollection of the two children scooping out the earth to form
a hollow has a remarkable parallel in the contemporary novel *Sula,* by
Toni Morrison, in which the activity denotes incipient sexuality cou-
pled with violence.[2] The nest image seems to have the same significance for Nelly and Hindley as it does for Heathcliff and Catherine.
As an archetypal image of feminine sexuality, it is ransacked, turned
into an image of destruction. Nelly's sight of hers and Hindley's childhood hollow filled with empty snail shells portends not only the death
of Hindley, as she feared, but the metaphorical "death" of her "son"
Hareton, who has turned against her and throws stones and abuse
when she tries to approach. Nelly's fantasy of a love relationship with
the father transforms, then, into the reality of hatred from the son.
The nest image in *Wuthering Heights* points to the men's fear of femininity. When Isabella escapes Heathcliff because her pregnancy awak-
ens a desire for self-preservation, she recognizes that her pregnant
state would be the greatest threat to him: "Do you think he could bear
to see me grow fat and merry . . . ?" she asks (208). The male characters' anxiety about feminine sexuality results, as we shall see in the
next chapter, in violent coercion of their bodies, and even in attempts
to extinguish femininity.

Joseph and Nelly, then, embody the values of the status quo in
Wuthering Heights. They both attempt to humiliate others into conventional behavior, and they use the Bible to shore up patriarchy's
devaluation of women.

7

Marking the Territory:
Heathcliff, Edgar, and Homosocial Desire

Wuthering Heights is universally regarded as a great love story; literary criticism, movies, songs, and even parodies have made much of the powerful passion between Heathcliff and Catherine, so that it seems almost preposterous to argue that *Wuthering Heights* is not primarily about love, or that the feelings between Heathcliff and Catherine arise from something other than spontaneous passion. However, if we look closely at the text, we will see that Heathcliff's love for Catherine is partly a consequence of, and is intimately bound up with, his rivalries with the other male characters, particularly Edgar. Furthermore, Heathcliff's relationships with women, especially Catherine, Isabella, and Cathy, are determined by his struggles with the men: the women come to represent his victories over his male rivals.

Although he is abusive towards the women and often physically violent, the critical and popular tradition has tended to heroize Heathcliff. Kettle argues that he retains our sympathies because there is moral justice in his revenge against his oppressors: he simply uses their weapons—"expropriation and property deals—against them" (*AK*, 140). I would add that women are a major "weapon" in Heathcliff's revenge, and that in *Wuthering Heights* it is the intense and passionate rivalry between the men which determines their relations with the women.

Patriarchal society depends on the traffic in, or exchange of, women: the anthropologist Levi-Strauss recognized that women, exchanged in marriage between kinship groups, function as signs of cooperation between men. Gayle Rubin developed this insight into the theory that social relations therefore depend upon the "traffic in women," and that the women's bodies are themselves signs of the exchange.[1] The comings and goings between Wuthering Heights and Thrushcross Grange illustrate Rubin's argument that women are "traffic" between men: Catherine marries Edgar and moves to Thrushcross Grange, Isabella is taken by Heathcliff to Wuthering Heights, and Cathy is incarcerated there and forced to marry Linton. Each marriage involves a brutal and total severance of other relations (Catherine from Heathcliff, Isabella from her brother, and Cathy from her father). Nelly, as the servant, is forced "much against my inclination" (because she has to abandon Hareton) to move to Thrushcross Grange with Catherine (129); later she goes back to Wuthering Heights, and then returns to the Grange again, all because of her mistresses' marriages. *Wuthering Heights* explores the effects that this "traffic" has on the women themselves.

If women are the objects of exchange between men, and relations between men form the basis of society, then it is a short step to Eve Sedgwick's view that relations between the sexes occur within a pervasive structure of desire between men:

> I will be using desire . . . not for a particular affective state or emotion, but for the affective or social force, the glue, even when its manifestation is hostility or hatred or something less emotively charged, that shapes an important relationship.[2]

Edgar and Heathcliff dramatically illustrate what Eve Sedgwick has named "homosocial desire,"—strong emotions which are not explicitly homosexual, and which may well be homophobic—between men. The confrontation between Heathcliff and Edgar in the kitchen at Thrushcross Grange, arguably the most decisive scene in the novel, is also the climax to Heathcliff's longstanding rivalry with his "masters." Heathcliff is linked by homosocial desire to Lockwood, Hindley, and Hareton, as well as Edgar. Even Charlotte Brontë in the "Preface" hints at the existence of homosocial desire (though of course she did not call it this); Heathcliff's one redeeming and humanizing characteristic is not, she says, his passion for Catherine as everyone assumes, but is rather his "rudely confessed regard for Hareton Earnshaw" (40). This chapter focuses on Heathcliff and Edgar as rivals, locked in attraction-repulsion to each other and in a triangular relation with Catherine.

The men's attitudes towards the women in *Wuthering Heights*, particularly their fear of feminine sexuality, is explicitly linked to their ways of reading, and their attitudes towards books and texts. The link between women and texts may not be immediately evident (very few people would connect the two), but we shall see that as "traffic," women do in fact function as texts: as signs of relationships between men. Whereas Edgar, like Lockwood, is presented as an avid reader, Heathcliff is never caught (with his trousers down) reading. He is, however, familiar with at least one literary genre: he is exasperated that Isabella persists "in picturing in me a hero of romance" and in expecting "chivalrous devotion" (187). Unlike Lockwood, Edgar and Hareton, Heathcliff does not treat books as though they were women; instead, he treats women as though they were texts. We shall see that he makes his mark—his unique and forcible signature—on Isabella, Catherine, and Cathy. Heathcliff's violence against women takes a specific form: he literally inscribes them with and as signs of his ownership, and therefore of his victory over his male rivals. We have already seen that for Lockwood the text is a woman; now we shall see that for Heathcliff the woman is a text.

Edgar certainly seems more benign than Heathcliff in his treatment of others. Yet Catherine blames Edgar as much as Heathcliff for her death; she is outraged that her husband buries himself in his library while she is dying. Heathcliff maintains that Edgar is incapable of understanding or truly loving Catherine; this is perhaps the case, but the question remains whether Heathcliff's "love" has any better consequences for Catherine's life.

HEATHCLIFF

Like Lockwood, Heathcliff continually forces exits and entries through doorways. Like Lockwood, his repeated and often violent encroachments of physical space parallel and symbolize assaults on the women. Heathcliff is forced to spend his first night at the Heights in the passageway, clearly indicating his outcast state (78). From then on, he attempts to exert control over latches, gates, and doorways. Thus Heathcliff's struggle with the "masters" of the Heights is symbolized by his relation to physical space: as Van de Laar observes of an early altercation with Hindley, the door is "a symbol of conflict" (*VL*, 133):

> ill-luck would have it that, as he opened the door leading from the kitchen on one side, Hindley opened it on the other; they met, and the master . . . shoved him back with a sudden thrust. (98)

In the very opening pages of the novel, it is Heathcliff who attempts to block Lockwood's entry to the Heights (45), and it is he who barges into Catherine's bedroom when Lockwood cries out in fear of the specter: "Hasty footsteps approached my chamber door: somebody pushed it open, with a vigorous hand" (68). Much later, when Heathcliff appears at Edgar's house after three years' absence, Nelly finds him with his "fingers on the latch, as if intending to open it for himself" (132); significantly, it is *he* who opens the door for Nelly. As time passes, Heathcliff's trespassing, in search of Catherine, becomes increasingly bold: "The open house was too tempting for Heathcliff to resist walking in: . . . He did not hit the right room directly . . . but he found it out ere I could reach the door" (194).

When Heathcliff disappears for three years, Joseph observes that "He's left th'yate ut t'full swing, and miss's pony has trodden dahn two rigs uh corn, un plottered through, raight o'er intuh t'meadow!" (124). The damage done by Catherine's pony is one among many examples (as we've seen) of animals as women's doubles in *Wuthering Heights*. Later, Heathcliff symbolically tries to reverse the damage when he attempts to hang Isabella's dog; in both cases the animals are the women's "familiars" (167). Not long after hanging Isabella's pet,

Heathcliff calls Isabella herself a bitch (188), and he later uses the same term for Cathy (72). Like Lockwood, Heathcliff unconsciously links women with animals, which adds an interesting dimension to Van de Laar's observation about the fight between Hindley and Heathcliff over the colts: "there is no sign of any love on the part of Heathcliff for his horse; he just wants to possess the best one" (*VL*, 175). I would argue that Heathcliff's relations with women are characterized by the same desire to "possess the best one."

Heathcliff's desire for Catherine coincides with hatred of his male oppressors. From the beginning Hindley provokes Heathcliff, regarding him as a "usurper of his parent's affections, and his privileges" (79). When Hindley, at his father's death, becomes the new "tyrannical" master of the house, he literally forces Heathcliff out:

> He drove him from their company to the servants, deprived him of the instructions of the curate, and insisted that he should labour out of doors instead. (87)

The children, says Nelly, become "reckless" in reaction to Heathcliff being ostracized; Catherine becomes Heathcliff's sole source of self-esteem and power. But Heathcliff does not express anything like love for Catherine until he witnesses the Lintons (including Edgar) admiring her: "I saw they were full of stupid admiration; she is so immeasurably superior to them—to everybody on earth; is she not, Nelly?" (92). Heathcliff's "love" for Catherine is inextricably tied to his being "thrown out" by the "masters" as unworthy of her company. When the two are caught looking in at the window of Thrushcross Grange, and Catherine is injured by the dog who is set upon them, she is retained, but Heathcliff is "dragged . . . into the garden," where he waits ready to shatter "their great glass panes to a million of fragments" if Catherine wants to be retrieved (91). Unfortunately, she doesn't, and here commence the dominating emotions of Heathcliff's life and the form that they take. His love for Catherine is inextricably tied to his envy of the Lintons and bitterness towards his class "superiors," and it kindles the desire to violently break barriers to get Catherine back. Furthermore, the image of Catherine behind a glass pane echoes Lockwood's nightmare, in which his shattering of a glass pane represents desire for, and fear of, sexual intercourse. It is not difficult to see Catherine and Heathcliff's visit to the Grange as a sort of rite of passage, signifying their transition from childhood into adolescence and sexual awareness. Heathcliff describes Catherine's assault by the Linton's dog in sexual terms:

> She did not yell out—no! She would have scorned to do it, if she had been spitted on the horns of a mad cow. . . . The dog was throttled off, his huge, purple tongue hanging half a foot out of his mouth, and his pendant lips streaming with bloody slaver. (90)

Catherine is "spitted" or pierced by an enormous pendulous tongue. In light of the fact that animals function throughout the text as "familiars" or representatives of their owners, it is clear that unconsciously, for Heathcliff, the incident at Thrushcross Grange represents losing Catherine to a sexual rival.

Very soon after this, Nelly observes that Heathcliff seems to "hate" Edgar "even then, as a rival" (99). On the same day—Christmas Day—Heathcliff begins to plot revenge on Hindley for belittling him in front of Edgar. Having been thrashed by Hindley for throwing hot apple sauce over Edgar, Heathcliff tells Nelly "I'm trying to settle how I shall pay Hindley back. I don't care how long I wait, if I can only do it, at last. I hope he will not die before I do!" (101).

Heathcliff's love for Catherine, then, is born with his hatred of Hindley and Edgar. Girard argues that the phenomenon of two men desiring the same woman (which abounds in Western Literature) is not caused by an accidental convergence of two desires on the same object, but rather is caused by rivalry between the two desires. The subject "will desire any object so long as he is convinced that it is already desired by another person whom he admires."[3] Thus, in loving the same woman, the rivals actually imitate each other: Girard claims that "mimetic" desire renders the antagonists increasingly alike; as the rivalry intensifies, so do their similarities. Sedgwick takes Girard's observations further to show that the rivalry between the men in a triangle takes the form of intense fascination, or "homosocial desire," which can be felt as loathing. Lin Haire-Sargent's recent novel *H: The Story of Heathcliff's Journey Back to Wuthering Heights* captures the homosocial desire between Heathcliff and Edgar: she imagines that in Heathcliff's three-year absence he accidentally encounters Edgar, and he writes to Catherine that his love for her became superimposed on his hatred for Edgar: "when I attempted to call up your face in my memory it resembled his—I could not keep the two apart:"

> So, by the day of his arrival I longed to see Edgar Linton . . . impatiently, intensely, as one might yearn, breath hitched in his throat, for the first glimpse of his lover.[4]

In Brontë's novel, however, Heathcliff and Edgar (more typically) recognize neither the inevitability of their both wanting Catherine, nor their similarity to each other. Nelly Dean, however, notes that they are complementary: "The contrast resembled what you see in exchanging a bleak, hilly, coal country for a beautiful fertile valley" (110). Each man has what the other painfully knows he lacks.

Heathcliff's jealousy is directed at Edgar's class: he believes that Edgar's birth, money, and status make him more desirable. Nelly tries to console Heathcliff with his masculinity: "You are younger, and yet, I'll be bound, you are taller and twice as broad across the shoulders— you could knock him down in a twinkling." Heathcliff retorts:

> "But, Nelly, if I knocked him down twenty times, that wouldn't make him less handsome, or me more so. I wish I had light hair and a fair skin, and was dressed, and behaved as well, and had a chance of being as rich as he will be!" (97).

"And cried for mamma, at every turn," retorts Nelly, "and trembled if a country lad heaved a fist against you, and stayed at home all day for a shower of rain" (97). Nelly and Heathcliff debate two stereotypes of masculinity: physical power and the power of money and position. Nelly declares that Edgar looks "quite a doll" beside Heathcliff (97), and emphasizes his lack of physical power. Lockwood observes that Edgar's portrait is "soft-featured . . . exceedingly resembling the young lady at the Heights," and that his figure is "almost too graceful"

(106–7). This feminine appearance, however, denotes, as Heathcliff recognizes, class superiority. Edgar (in the words of Gilbert and Gubar)

> does not need a strong, conventionally masculine body, because his mastery is contained in books, wills, testaments, leases, titles, rent-rolls, documents, languages, all the paraphernalia by which patriarchal culture is transmitted from one generation to the next. (*G&G*, 281)

Thus Brontë explicitly places Edgar's and Heathcliff's "love" for Catherine in the context of their struggle over power, property, and sexuality. Their fight over Catherine is a fight for masculinity as defined by patriarchal society.

Irigaray points out that "the circulation of women among men is what establishes the operations of society, at least of patriarchal society," so that "the constitution of women as 'objects,' " represents "the materialization of relations among men" (*TS*, 184–85). If the proprietorship of the houses, Thrushcross Grange and Wuthering Heights, is proof of masculine social status and power, the proprietorship of the women is proof of masculine sexuality. Although Heathcliff wins Wuthering Heights from Hindley at cards (222–23), Thrushcross Grange involves the brutal seductions of Isabella and Cathy.

Heathcliff's interest in Isabella is entirely mercenary. When Catherine tells Heathcliff that her sister-in-law is infatuated with him, he asks "She's her brother's heir is she not?" He also coolly declares that:

> "You'd hear of odd things, if I lived alone with that mawkish, waxen face; the most ordinary would be painting on its white the colours of the rainbow, and turning the blue eyes black, every day or two." (145)

These chilling intentions towards Isabella encapsulate the nature of the violence in *Wuthering Heights*. Heathcliff regards Isabella's face as a white canvas on which he literally will make his mark. I commented earlier that for Heathcliff women are texts, visible signs of his ownership and victories over other men. His violence towards Isabella is for "nothing more," says Naomi Jacobs, "than her resemblance to her brother."[5] But this is the point: Heathcliff marries Isabella to revenge himself against Edgar, but he hits her in order to transform her into a visual sign of his victory over his rival.

We discussed in the introduction how exchanging a woman in marriage turns her, as Elizabeth Bronfen argues, into "a sign referring to something more and something other than her corporality."[6] The exchange of the woman, I have added, also represents a tacit agreement between the men to read the woman *as* a sign. This perhaps explains Edgar's troubling acquiesence in his sister's abduction by Heathcliff:

> "She went of her own accord. . . . She had a right to go if she pleased—Trouble me no more about her—hereafter she is only my sister in name: not because I disown her, but because she has disowned me." (170)

Edgar seems to regard Isabella as a fallen woman, because she has taken it upon herself to dispose of her own body according to her own desires, thus co-opting the male family members' right to exchange her as they see fit. Edgar washes his hands of Isabella because he is unwilling to admit defeat at Heathcliff's hands.

When Heathcliff abducts Isabella, he hangs her dog Fanny (the name is slang for the female genitals); Nelly finds it "at its last gasp" (167). Although Heathcliff does not strangle his wife (if he did, she would no longer serve to represent his masculinity), his sadism links her in his mind with her "brach" or bitch:

> "Now, was it not the depth of absurdity—of genuine idiocy, for that pitiful, slavish, mean-minded brach to dream that I could love her? . . . I've sometimes relented, from pure lack of invention, in my experiments on what she could endure, and still creep shamefully cringing back!" (188)

Heathcliff is quite open about his intention of abusing Isabella to the point at which her insanity would deprive her of rights to her own person:

> "If you are called upon in a court of law, you'll remember her language, Nelly! And take a good look at that countenance—she's near the point which would suit me. No, you're not fit to be your own guardian, Isabella, now; and I, being your legal protector, must retain you in my custody, however distasteful the obligation may be." (188–89)

Heathcliff wants Edgar to know about the abuse: "But tell him, also, to set his fraternal and magisterial heart at ease, that I keep strictly within the limits of the law" (188).

The violence against the women in *Wuthering Heights* is frequently directed at the head, and two of the most vivid examples focus on the mouth: Hindley tries to force a knife down Nelly's throat, and Heathcliff hits Cathy so hard that her mouth fills with blood (114, 313). These violent incidents are clearly sexualized: the lips, as Irigaray explains in "When Our Lips Speak Together," frequently symbolize female genitalia (*TS*, 205–18). Juliet McMaster has perceptively demonstrated that when Heathcliff forces Cathy to marry his son Linton, he also symbolically consummates the union for him.[7] Linton recounts to Nelly (while sucking a stick of candy) that after the marriage, Heathcliff had asserted his son's marital rights over Cathy's property and her body: when she attempted to retain the half of the locket containing her father Edgar's portrait, Heathcliff "struck her down, and wrenched it off the chain, and crushed it with his foot" (313). As Van de Laar comments, Heathcliff sees in the portrait "a projection of his own hatred towards Edgar, and the act of crushing it is equivalent to the subjection of a hated enemy" (*VL*, 137). But this is not all; Heathcliff's violence against Cathy is another example of inscribing the woman as "traffic" in the homosocial order. He deflowers her at the same time as he forces her to replace her birth father with a new one—himself. "When papa was gone," says Linton,

> "she made me come to the window and showed me her cheek cut on the inside, against her teeth, and her mouth filling with blood . . . she has never spoken to me since; and I sometimes think she can't speak for pain." (313)

Cathy's silence only enhances her function as a sign; like Isabella, she too is marked as an object of exchange. "Every . . . day," says Irigaray,

> the head of the family has to re-insure his potency. Every single day, therefore, he is enjoined to reappropriate the right to exploit blood and then, as a result, to go on to more sublime pursuits. (*SW*, 126)

In other words, the patriarch's sense of self depends upon the oppression, even the blood, of others.

Although there is no scene in which Heathcliff strikes Catherine, he does mark her with bruises just before her death. Nelly sees Heathcliff make "four distinct impressions left blue in the colourless skin" (195). Once again the image is that of inscribing a blank surface with marks—marks of ownership. As Irigaray says of women before entering "the market" of patriarchal exchange, they have not yet lost their "candid whiteness," by being inscribed with the "dead blood, black blood" of the marks of ownership (*TS*, 207). Irigaray links the black blood of marked women to the phallocentric texts which circulate in patriarchal culture:

> Perhaps blood will have the freedom . . . to circulate, only if it takes the form of ink. The pen will always already have been dipped into the murdered bodies of the mother and the woman and will write in black, in black blood (like) ink, the clotting of its (his?) desires and pleasures. (*SW*, 126)

In other words, texts which circulate in society, which frequently figure femininity as lacking, as a "gap," are a manifestation of patriarchy's violent repression of women. Although Catherine appears to suffer less physical abuse at the hands of Heathcliff than either Isabella or Cathy, it could be argued that she pays the biggest price for his revenge. The dog which Heathcliff hangs to symbolize his abduction of Isabella, and hatred for the Lintons, is discovered at the Grange just before the onset of Catherine's illness (167). The strangled dog thus links Catherine and Isabella as Heathcliff's victims. Kavanagh argues that Heathcliff's treatment of Isabella is "a grotesque parody of his obsessive pursuit of Cathy. . . . Isabella pays only a more immediate and acute price than Cathy for her attraction to Heathcliff" (*JK*, 66–67). While Heathcliff's relationship with Isabella can be seen as a grotesque exaggeration of his relationship with Catherine, it isn't at all clear that Isabella pays a bigger price than Catherine for being attracted to Heathcliff. Isabella confirms this by declaring (after Catherine's death) that Catherine "would have been living now, had it not been for Mr. Heathcliff. After all, it is preferable to be hated than loved by him" (216).

Catherine herself accuses Heathcliff (and Edgar) of killing her. She dies (as we shall see in the following chapter) as a direct result of refusing to choose whose property she shall be, refusing to be exchanged by them. Catherine's self-starvation can be seen as an attempt to control her own body in the face of Edgar's and Heathcliff's fight for ownership of it; ironically, she dies in the attempt. Heathcliff's revenge on the men involves violence not against them, but rather against their women. As Bronfen says:

> It is significant that the form revenge most often takes is the transformation of a woman's body into a sign, by others and by herself. The point where violence enters into the exchange also forms the link between the institutionalising action of exogamy, which turns Woman into a commodity, and the cultural project of representation, which turns her into a trope. (*EB*, 227)

In other words, the very same (violent) process which turns woman into an object of exchange also turns her into a sign, a text. In *Wuthering Heights* the women's bodies, not the men's, bear the brunt of the effects of a homosocial order. Although the novel *H: The Story of Heathcliff's Journey Back to Wuthering Heights* cleverly recognizes the existence of homosocial desire between Heathcliff and Edgar, it lapses into grotesque absurdity when Heathcliff (who is adept at gelding horses) surgically removes one of Edgar's testicles while Edgar is unconscious (having just saved his life). Heathcliff presents the testicle to Edgar saying:

> "Stop blubbering and listen, . . . I took off only one. I have left you half a man. . . . I have left one *in situ* for a reason. . . . As I told you

> earlier, you will drop your suit of Catherine Earnshaw. . . . You must
> either give up Cathy's company, favor, conversation, caresses, and et
> cetera (and even to your puny passions this must be a mighty blow);
> or, should you persist, become a full gelding in time for your wed-
> ding night." (*H-S*, 201–2)

Perhaps the ridiculousness of this passage is partly due to the literal-
ization of Heathcliff's attempt in *Wuthering Heights* to emasculate
Edgar; but perhaps it is also because the violence takes the form of
one man castrating another, which does not fit the logic either of
homosociality (which "castrates" *women*) or of *Wuthering Heights*. In
Wuthering Heights it is the *women's* bodies that are maimed as signs of
the interpretive agreement between the men. The woman's body as a
signifier is deprived of the signified "woman": Catherine and Isabella
disappear into death. The men's need for mutual recognition, their
pursuit of dominance, costs the women (with the exception of Cathy)
their lives.

EDGAR

Although Heathcliff is cruel and exploitative, readers and critics
almost always prefer him to Edgar. Many critics, including feminists,
find him irresistible, and Moser even goes so far as to argue that
"Heathcliff's presence was vital to the conception of all three children
of the second generation" (*TM*, 16).[8] In contrast to Heathcliff's viril-
ity, Edgar is usually regarded as effeminate, his softness and passivity
amounting to ineffectuality. Although Edgar is the "good guy," readers almost always prefer the "bad guy" Heathcliff (*F/R*, 76).[9]

Doubtless the imagery associated with Edgar in *Wuthering
Heights* contributes to his lack of attractiveness. Catherine uses
metaphor to attempt to explain how she and Heathcliff differ from
Edgar: "Whatever our souls are made of, his and mine are the same,
and Linton's is as different as moonbeam from lightning, or frost from
fire" (121). Whereas Catherine and Heathcliff are associated with
dynamic images of transcendence—on a "vertical axis," as Van de

Laar says (*VL*, 51)—Edgar is associated with images of stasis (on a horizontal axis, we could say); Edgar's greatest happiness demonstrates his desire for stability and even petrifaction: anticipating death, he tells Nelly that he has been

> happy musing by myself among those stones, under that old church—lying, through the long June evenings, on the green mound of [Catherine's] grave, and wishing, yearning for the time, when I might lie beneath it. (289)

Edgar's "passivity," says Van de Laar, is "matched by the flatness of the language in which he expresses his longing" (*VL*, 103). As we shall see, Edgar's inability to express his emotions makes him in that respect more typically "masculine" than Heathcliff. His love for Catherine is expressed as a wish to "have [her] under this roof" (171).

This would be an insignificant remark were it not for the fact that Edgar's (unsuccessful) attempts to control and constrain his wife and daughter take the form of attempts to keep them under his roof. The conflict with Catherine during her climactic illnesses is played out through the opening and closing of doors and windows: "He shuts the window, cutting off her communication with the moor and therefore with life itself" (*VL*, 141). Edgar also tries to keep his daughter Cathy within the bounds of Thrushcross Grange, a restraint which, we shall see in chapter 10, prompts her defiance. Despite his apparent mildness, Edgar confines, literally reins in, the women in his life. Edgar's relationship to Catherine is described by Nelly as that of a honeysuckle wrapped around a thorn (131); Catherine is the hard and prickly thorn, and Edgar is the honeysuckle, conveying, says Van de Laar, the idea of "limpness" (*VL*, 180). The sexual innuendo, though doubtlessly unintended, is unmistakable.

If Edgar is limp, Heathcliff is a prick. But the prick, says Jane Gallop, is transparent; therefore in some ways less insidious than the disguised misogynist. Because "the prick obviously gets pleasure from his cruelty," he "exposes" himself, and thereby forfeits some of his patriarchal power.[10] "The phallic role," says Gallop, "demands impassivity." In that case, Edgar's unimpassioned and unimaginative "rigid authority" is ultimately more insidious than Heathcliff's obvious bullying. Edgar attempts at all times to control himself as well as others. Heathcliff gnashes his teeth and foams "like a mad dog" (197), weeps, raves, trembles all over, knocks his head against a tree until it bleeds (204), and continually voices his anger, pain, and grief. He is brutally honest to the end. He tells the dying Catherine: "I have not one word of comfort—you deserve this. You have killed yourself" (197); yet minutes later he is weeping (198).

Edgar, on the other hand, is humiliated by any evidence of his own emotions. In the climactic confrontation between Heathcliff and Edgar in the kitchen of the Grange, Catherine locks them all in and throws the key in the fire,

> whereupon Mr. Edgar was taken with a nervous trembling, and his countenance grew deadly pale. For his life he could not avert that access of emotion—mingled anguish and humiliation overcame him completely. He leant on the back of a chair, and covered his face. (153–54)

It seems that Edgar's anguish is caused not so much by his wife siding with Heathcliff, as by his own inability to control his emotions. At one of the most crucial moments in his life, when his relationship with Catherine is most threatened, Edgar expresses his "love" with: "I absolutely *require* to know which you choose" (156). If "the phallic role demands impassivity," then Edgar's rigidity is more "phallic" than Heathcliff's emotionalism.

Although Gilbert and Gubar recognize Edgar's "power and status" as the "power of the patriarch," they find the following metaphor of his attraction to Catherine "odd" (*G&G*, 282). During his courtship of Catherine, Edgar threatens to leave after she slaps his face; he hesitates, and the text observes:

> The soft thing looked askance through the window—he possessed the power to depart, as much as a cat possesses the power to leave a mouse half killed, or a bird half eaten. (112)

Gilbert and Gubar conclude that the somewhat contradictory metaphor of victim and victimizer is appropriate after all, because Edgar
represents the "devouring force that will gnaw and worry Catherine to
death" (*G&G*, 282).

In fact both Edgar and Heathcliff "worry Catherine to death." In
their fight over Catherine, she is just like the little dog almost pulled in
two by Isabella and Edgar (89). We shall see that Catherine is right in
her accusation:

> "You and Edgar have broken my heart, Heathcliff! and you both
> come to bewail the deed to me, as if you were the people to be
> pitied! I shall not pity you, not I. You have killed me—and thriven
> on it, I think." (195)

In the same way that Heathcliff marries Isabella "on purpose" to "provoke Edgar to desperation," Edgar and Heathcliff pursue Catherine to
"provoke" each other "to desperation" (188). Even in their most
intense moments of "love" for Catherine, neither Edgar nor Heathcliff
can forget each other; in fact, each depends on a comparison with the
other to validate the sincerity of his own love. Heathcliff, denying his
desire to "exasperate or insult Mr. Linton" by pursuing Catherine
(189), argues that Edgar is an

> "insipid, paltry creature attending her from *duty* and *humanity*!
> From *pity* and *charity*! He might as well plant an oak in a flower-
> pot, and expect it to thrive, as imagine he can restore her to vigour
> in the soil of his shallow cares!" (190).

Conversely, Edgar's first thought when he sees the dying Catherine, is
of himself in relation to Heathcliff: " 'Catherine what have you done?'
commenced the master. 'Am I nothing to you, any more? Do you love
that wretch, Heath—'" (165).

It seems that Catherine is right in accusing Edgar of indifference
and insensiblity—of having "veins . . . full of ice-water" (156). After the
terrible confrontation which makes Catherine ill, "Mr. Linton . . . spent
his time in the library, and did not inquire concerning his wife's occupations" (157). The text repeats no less than *seven* times (157, 8, 9, 60,

64, 66) that during Catherine's last illness Edgar shuts himself up with his books. "What in the name of all that feels, has he to do with *books*, when I am dying?" (160), cries Catherine. She advises him to "return to your books . . . I'm glad you possess a consolation, for all you had in me is gone" (165–66). The fact that Edgar replaces the dying Catherine with books suggests that he too, like Lockwood and Heathcliff, makes unconscious connections between women and texts. This is made explicit by Nelly, who reproaches Catherine that Edgar "is continually among his books, since he *has no other society*" (159; emphasis mine). But Edgar finds consolation "among books that he never opened" (158). Perhaps this is because, like Lockwood, he is as afraid to open the texts as he is to "open" Catherine (emotionally and physically). Perhaps it is because he recognizes that he and Heathcliff between them have turned Catherine herself into a text—a signifier deprived of its signified. The last time we see Catherine she is a lifeless form being exchanged between the two men: "the other stopped all demonstrations, at once, by placing the lifeless-looking form in his arms" (199).

The homosocial desire between Heathcliff and Edgar verges on homoeroticism when it climaxes (as it were) in the back-kitchen (which is symbolic of the anus in Victorian domestic topography) of the Grange. The fight is explicitly over "property," but it is unclear whether Edgar is defending his wife or his house from Heathcliff's "contaminating" influence:

> "Your presence is a moral poison that would contaminate the most virtuous—for that cause, and to prevent worse consequences, I shall deny you, hereafter, admission into this house, and give notice, now, that I require your instant departure. Three minutes' delay will render it involuntary and ignominious." (153)

Apart from being a very verbose way of saying "get out or I'll have you thrown out," Edgar is denying Heathcliff access to his property (whether Catherine or the Grange); indeed, Catherine's "propriety," or sexual morality, is thrown into question by her willingness to encourage Heathcliff: "what notion of propriety must you have to remain here . . . ?" her husband asks (152).

Catherine's reaction reveals that she experiences the fight between Heathcliff and Egdar as a violation of herself. First she accuses her husband of listening at the door in a way that implies his cowardice and impotence:

> "Have you been listening at the door, Edgar?" asked the mistress, in a tone particularly calculated to provoke her husband, implying both carelessness and contempt of his irritation. (152)

Then she tries to seize control of the space by locking them all in and throwing the key on the fire; and finally, she cries to Edgar "We are vanquished! we are vanquished!" (153–54). The fight, which is conducted at the hearth (an archetypal feminine space), and through the opening and closing of doors, is clearly a bid for Catherine. In response, Catherine threatens to swallow the house key, showing that she at least recognizes the connection between the property and her body (153). In asserting the right to stand on the hearth, both men seem willing to fight to the death. It would not be going too far to say this is a symbolic gang rape, in which both men try to force themselves on Catherine. Why, asks Irigaray, does the male fantasy of desirable femininity require

> *a closed, solid, virginal body to be forced open*? . . . In this view, the body's pleasure always results from a forced entry—preferably bloody—into an *enclosure*. A *property*? (TS, 201)

After striking Heathcliff, Edgar "walked out by the back door into the yard, and from thence, to the front entrance," as though to re-establish his stronghold (154). Employing phallic images of masculine power, Catherine warns Heathcliff that Edgar will "return with a brace of pistols," and Nelly that three men are returning each armed with "a bludgeon" (154). Heathcliff, after refusing to "cross the threshold" until he has "floored" Edgar, has second thoughts, and retaliates by escaping with his own phallic weapon: "He seized the poker, smashed the lock from the inner door, and made his escape as they tramped in" (155).

Thus the climax of the triangular relationship between Heathcliff, Edgar, and Catherine is not only violent but also sexualized, and Catherine reacts as though she has indeed been raped. Two months later she dies.

Peter Miles claims that the narrative of *Wuthering Heights* is one of "property ownership, centered on Heathcliff" (*PM*, 63), and he invokes Nelly's declaration that her tale is a "cuckoo's" history. The cuckoo invades the nest; but the "nest," the property that Heathcliff appropriates from his rivals, is not merely the houses. As we shall explore further in the following chapters, the "nest" that Heathcliff violates is also that of feminine integrity.

8

Beyond Property:
Catherine's Articulation
of a Feminine "Excess"

The critical tradition of *Wuthering Heights* concentrates almost entirely on Heathcliff at the expense of Catherine. Even a feminist critic, Patricia Yaeger, claims that "all of us, at one time or another, have identified with Heathcliff's victimization, with his gorgeous, sadistic rage" (*PY*, 203). Yet, if our reluctance to focus on Catherine resembles Lockwood piling up "the books in a pyramid" to keep out Catherine's ghost, and stopping his ears against her pleas to be let in, then the whole novel can be seen to be about this fearful rejection of Catherine's ghost (67). Admitting Catherine to the center of our critical vision results, I am attempting to demonstrate, in a significant rethinking of the entire novel. Catherine's ghost, as Musselwhite suggests, upsets the "common sense" readings of the critical establishment (*DM*, 155). What Musselwhite calls the "unread and outcast text" of *Wuthering Heights*—its unacknowledged message—is not so much Catherine as a ghost, however, but what the ghost signifies, which is Catherine (and all women) as text (*DM*, 155). We have seen that Heathcliff and Edgar turn Catherine into a sign of their homosocial relationship, and that all the women in the novel function as signs of masculinity. This chapter illustrates Catherine's resistance to becoming an object of property, and to being turned into a document of the men's struggle for power. Ironically, Catherine's resistance costs her her life, but (as we shall see in chapter 10), her daughter Cathy continues the effort to subvert patriarchal dominance.

The men do not finally succeed in turning women into "nowt," as Joseph puts it (57). Catherine's ghost, which early in the novel "personifies" from her marginalia, goes on to haunt the entire text of *Wuthering Heights* (69). Wendy Craik points out that

> There can be few novels in which the heroine dies less than half-way through; there can be few heroines whose passion so permeates all its pages.[1]

This echoes Heathcliff's observation after Catherine's death that the whole world of the novel is "a dreadful collection of memoranda" of her presence (353). Catherine paradoxically is omnipresent in the novel by virtue of her absence. Her ghost, that terrifying specter that appears in the gaps of Lockwood's phallocentric reading, is the femininity that will not be denied.

Catherine's diary offers an alternative reading strategy to that adopted by Lockwood and the other men. Lockwood is usually regarded as the only surrogate reader in *Wuthering Heights*, yet we've seen how the novel exposes his efforts to "penetrate" a text as a sublimation of his sexual conflicts. Catherine is an equally important, yet almost wholly overlooked, surrogate reader in *Wuthering Heights*. Her diary offers an alternative feminine reading strategy to Lockwood's masculine one: where he attempts to "penetrate" the text, Catherine envelops it in her own discourse; where he is terrified by what may be found in the gaps, she inhabits them. Catherine's diary challenges not only the patriarchal "tomes" in which she writes, but also the reader's awareness of what has been repressed by those canonical books of Western culture (62). Catherine's diary, in the words of Luce Irigaray, articulates the repressed femininity of the texts of patriarchy. Because "representation" is "determined by male subjects," the feminine must be deciphered as inter-dict: within the signs or between them, between the realized meanings, between the lines . . . (*SW*, 22)

    Catherine's diary embodies her social and authorial status, representing simultaneously her repression and her resistance. Catherine's story is the record of hysteria. Irigaray maintains that all women in patriarchal society are to a degree hysterical; the term is not intended to be pejorative, because women internalize ideals of femininity which are nevertheless impossible to fulfill, placing them in a frustratingly conflicted position (*TS*, 136–38; *SW*, 71–72). Catherine's society expects her to be docile, pious, dependent, and domesticated. Women cannot evade, says Irigaray, their society's ideology of femininity, and yet at the same time they cannot avoid transgressing it; thus they are are always "implicated in it and at the same time exceeding its limits" (*TS*, 163). Catherine's diary articulates, in form as well as content, the ways in which her needs and desires exceed what is deemed acceptably feminine. As a child, for example, she should have been seen and not heard, whereas "she was never so happy as when we were all scolding her at once, and she defying us with her bold, saucy look, and her ready words" (83–84). As a teenager, she should not have enjoyed romping on the moors with a "gypsy brat" who was supposed to be a servant (77). And as a young woman she should not have expected to marry Edgar Linton and remain intimate with Heathcliff. Catherine's diary and her life represent, Irigaray would say, a "*disruptive excess* . . . on the feminine side" (*TS*, 78). Because a woman's "desires . . . find themselves reduced to silence in terms of a culture that does not allow them to be expressed" (*TS*, 136), they must be voiced through but beyond the ideology of femininity that defines her. Catherine attempts to conduct her life in a manner that is consistent with her practice of writing in the margins, but no one, not even Heathcliff, will listen to what she tries to say. The major decision of Catherine's life, to marry Edgar while still loving Heathcliff, can be seen as an attempt to remain in a liminal position, between the two men, rather than belonging to one or the other. In her effort to avoid being the property of either Edgar or Heathcliff, and in order to exert control over her own body, Catherine resorts to what we now call "anorexia nervosa." Her hysterical illness, which finally proves fatal, is the climax to the contradictory position which she attempts to live. Catherine, more than anyone else in the novel, embodies a critique of the status quo, of a society which depends for its existence on the circulation of women's bodies.

Catherine's last illness is the culmination of not only her conflicts with Edgar and Heathcliff, but also the life-long tension (of which her relations are a manifestation) caused by her simultaneous conformity and rebellion. In an unwittingly perceptive observation, Nelly says that Catherine was "led . . . to adopt a double character without exactly intending to deceive any one" (107). Irigaray would reply that the assumption of this double character is inevitable, because Catherine internalizes impossible expectations. Catherine's father declares that he "rues" that he ever "reared" her because she is naughtier than her brother (84). Like Maggie Tulliver in George Eliot's *The Mill on the Floss,* Catherine, being the girl, is the badge of the family's respectability, and should not step out of line. When she is caught at Thrushcross Grange the Lintons call her a "hatless savage," equating a lack of feminine decorum and dress with lack of white Western "civilized" values. Furthermore, they blame the male members of the family for allowing her "heathenism":

> "Miss Earnshaw scouring the country with a gipsy!" . . . "What culpable carelessness in her brother! . . . that he lets her grow up in absolute heathenism." (91)

Catherine is what we used to call a "tomboy." The first thing we learn about her is that at six years old she chooses, as a gift from her father, "a whip" (77), a symbol of phallic power and control.

When Nelly calls Catherine a "haughty headstrong creature!" (106) "with her bold, saucy look, and her ready words" (83–84), she implies that Catherine's verbal and oracular "looseness" indicates sexual "looseness." Both Catherine's and Cathy's "bold saucy look" has been brilliantly analyzed by Beth Newman. She argues that when these women look back (as they frequently do) at the men who look at

them, they threaten male dominance: "the woman's look is represented as provoking, withering, annihilating" (*BN*, 1032). When a
woman returns the gaze, "she asserts her 'existence' as a subject, her
place outside the position of object to which the male gaze relegates
her" (*BN*, 1032). The ways in which the male characters in *Wuthering
Heights* respond to the female gaze demonstrates, Newman argues,
male castration anxiety. Cathy has an "evil eye" which she directs at
men (57); when she stares at Lockwood, for example, he finds it
"exceedingly embarrassing and disagreeable" (52). The woman who
returns the gaze "is dangerous to men," because she assumes the masculine role of being actively sexual (*BN*, 1032).

Catherine's "bold, saucy look"—her refusal of deferential femininity—is implicitly punished, though not fully remedied, by the dog
bite and convalescence at Thrushcross Grange. When she and Heathcliff are caught looking through the window of the Grange, Mr. Linton regards it as insubordination and even emasculation: "To beard a
magistrate in his stronghold, and on the Sabbath, too! where will their
insolence stop?" (90). Heathcliff gets off relatively lightly, whereas
Catherine is attacked by a dog in a manner strongly suggestive, as we
discussed in the last chapter, of rape: "his huge, purple tongue hanging half a foot out of his mouth, and his pendant lips streaming with
bloody slaver" (90). After a symbolic violent sexual initiation, Catherine is retained at the Grange and subjected to a program of feminization, primarily by other women. Linton's wife "reform[s]" Catherine,
and undertakes "to keep her . . . in due restraint . . . employing art,
not force" (92). Through "fine clothes and flattery," Catherine is
taught to be looked at rather than to look (93). What Nelly calls
Catherine's "double character" originates at Thrushcross Grange
where, as she submits to having her feet washed, her hair combed, and
a plate of cakes emptied into her lap, she continues to tease the dog
that had attacked her (92). Catherine simultaneously submits and yet
resists all that the Lintons represent.

Five weeks later Catherine ostensibly has become a young lady:

> Instead of a wild, hatless little savage jumping into the house, and
> rushing to squeeze us all breathless, there lighted from a handsome
> black pony a very dignified person, with brown ringlets falling from

the cover of a feathered beaver, and a long cloth habit which she was
obliged to hold up with both hands that she might sail in. (93)

Hindley "delightedly" observes that Catherine is "quite a beauty! I
should scarcely have known you—you look like a lady now" (93).
Catherine can no longer touch the dogs, hug Nelly, or even remove
her own hat, for fear of spoiling her appearance (93). She is no longer
a "wild, hatless little savage"; her gender, class, and racial characteristics pointedly contrast with Heathcliff's:

> Nobody . . . even did him the kindness to call him a dirty boy, and
> bid him wash himself, once a week. . . . Therefore, not to mention
> his clothes, which had seen three months' service, in mire and dust,
> and his thick uncombed hair, the surface of his face and hands was
> dismally beclouded. He might well skulk behind the settle, on
> beholding such a bright, graceful damsel enter the house, instead of a
> rough-headed counterpart to himself, as he expected. (94)

Catherine is dismayed by Heathcliff's dirtiness: "Why, how very black
and cross you look! and how—how funny and grim!" (94). Heathcliff
refuses to shake hands when Hindley turns it into a sign of his class
inferiority: " 'Shake hands, Heathcliff,' said Mr. Earnshaw, conde-
scendingly; 'once in a way, that is permitted' " (94). Catherine is dismayed:

> "I did not mean to laugh at you . . . I could not hinder myself.
> Heathcliff, shake hands, at least! What are you sulky for? It was only
> that you looked odd—If you wash your face, and brush your hair it
> will be all right. But you are so dirty!" (94)

Catherine hopes that a little water will wash away the differences
between herself and Heathcliff, but the detailed contrast between their
appearances suggests that inscribed on their bodies are significant differences in class, gender, and even race. Leonore Davidoff describes
how, in the nineteenth century,

> [m]iddle-class children not only learned that certain social spaces
> belonged to certain social groups, they also learned to use their

bodies to express class and gender boundaries. Little ladies and gen-
tlemen did not sit on steps; they stood absolutely straight; they did
not whistle, scuff, or slouch. By imitating middle-class adults they
learned habits of command through silent body-language, through
the way they looked at people, through tone of voice as well as
accent. (*LD*, 97)

When Catherine shows concern for her hands and dress after touching
Heathcliff, he snatches his hand away, and dashes from the room, saying: "You needn't have touched me . . . I shall be as dirty as I please,
and I like to be dirty, and I will be dirty" (95), thus emphasizing by
repetition that "dirt" on the body signifies his difference. Nelly brings
to the surface the underlying racism of the play on Heathcliff's "black-
ness": " 'a good heart will help you to a bonny face, my lad,' I continued, 'if you were a regular black' " (98). Seeing the extent to which he
is alienated from Catherine, Heathcliff later repents by having his face
washed and his hair combed: "Nelly, make me decent," he says, "I'm
going to be good." (96). Catherine's transformation at Thrushcross
Grange is much more than a transition into adulthood. It is an attempt
at "separating the two friends," to facilitate Catherine's indoctrina-
tion—which Nelly calls a "plan of reform"—into desirable middle-
class femininity (93). From this point on Catherine adopts the "double
character" necessitated by her conflicting needs for acceptance and
freedom, expressed by her need for intimacy with both Heathcliff and
Edgar (107). While "Heathcliff kept his hold on her affections unal-
terably" (106), Catherine "took care not to act like him" among those
who called him "a 'vulgar young ruffian,' and 'worse than a brute'"
(107).

Catherine's decision to marry Edgar represents her recognition
of the impossibility of escaping the conventions of middle-class wom-
anhood: she regards Edgar as a means to respectability for herself.
Although Nelly exaggerates when she says that Edgar is an "acquisi-
tion" which answers Catherine's "ambition" (107), her facetious sum-
mary of Catherine's reasons for choosing him does emphasize certain
characteristics which Heathcliff lacks: "You love Mr. Edgar because
he is handsome, and young, and cheerful, and rich, and loves you"

(119). Edgar answers to the needs of Catherine's socialized self, whereas Heathcliff is a projection of the part of herself that will not submit to socialization: his indifference to appearance and scorn of politeness are a reflection of Catherine's own repressed desires. Like Heathcliff, Catherine is "haughty" and "headstrong," and however hard she tries, Nelly cannot "bring down her arrogance" (106). Catherine tries to explain her decision to marry Edgar through a dream. She tells Nelly, the reluctant listener, that she dreamt she was in (a very conventional) heaven, but that,

> "heaven did not seem to be my home; and I broke my heart with weeping to come back to earth; and the angels were so angry that they flung me out, into the middle of the heath on top of Wuthering Heights, where I woke sobbing for joy. That will do to explain my secret, as well as the other. I've no more business to marry Edgar Linton than I have to be in heaven." (120–21)

Catherine prefers the heath to heaven, and the Heights to the Grange: her dream is a clear expression of her desire to range free in the marginal spaces of the moors and her diary.

The psychoanalyst Jacques Lacan sees desire as the product of socialization: it is that which is left over after our entry into social existence. Our desire cannot be clearly or fully articulated because our assimilation into society means that we can confidently express only that which is socially sanctioned. Desire is that which survives in excess of what can be said in a particular culture.[2] While Catherine's love for Edgar effects her assimilation into the dominant class and values of her society, her continued love for Heathcliff, like her writing in her diary, represents that which is in excess of her assimilation. Catherine finds it very difficult to put into words what Heathcliff means to her, except that he represents everything in her that is enduring:

> "My love for Heathcliff resembles the eternal rocks beneath—a source of little visible delight, but necessary. Nelly, I *am* Heathcliff—he's always, always in my mind—not as a pleasure, any more than I am always a pleasure to myself—but as my own being—so, don't talk of our separation again—it is impracticable; and—" (122)

Catherine's famous assertion "I *am* Heathcliff" is not an indication that she depends on him for her identity, as critics have claimed, but rather as Stevenson argues, the reverse (*JS*, 72). Heathcliff is a projection of Catherine's unconscious desires (*JS*, 72).

When Catherine declares that Heathcliff "comprehends in his person my feelings to Edgar and myself," she is right insofar as Heathcliff is her own construction (122). As a projection of her unconscious self, he embraces or includes her attraction for Edgar. But Catherine is sadly mistaken if she means by "comprehend" that Heathcliff as a separate entity will *understand* either her love for Edgar or her "excessive" unconventional desires. In this respect Heathcliff proves to be as conventional as Edgar: neither man can fathom Catherine's need to love both and to belong to neither. Heathcliff betrays Catherine by lapsing into a struggle with Edgar for ownership of her body. Catherine regards relationships very differently; she seems to mean it when she tells Heathcliff that she is not jealous of him marrying Isabella, and she refuses to forfeit her intimacy with Heathcliff for her husband's peace of mind (150, 156).

The bid for Catherine's body reaches its climax, as we have seen, when Heathcliff and Edgar confront each other in the back-kitchen of the Grange, but we have not yet considered this episode from Catherine's point of view (152–55). Catherine is furious that her husband should question her virtue and is indignant with both men:

> "No, I'll swallow the key before you shall get it! I'm delightfully rewarded for my kindness to each! After constant indulgence of one's weak nature, and the other's bad one, I earn, for thanks, two samples of blind ingratitude, stupid to absurdity! Edgar, I was defending you and yours; and I wish Heathcliff may flog you sick, for daring to think an evil thought of me!" (153)

Catherine, as we've seen, tries to seize control over the property and her own body by threatening to swallow the key. The men may use "bludgeons" and "a poker" to force entry and exit, but Catherine ultimately holds "the key" to herself; neither of them can have her.

Despite Catherine's disgust at their tussle, the men continue to press her to make a decision. She can escape only by removing herself, first psychologically into madness, and then physically by starving herself out of existence. The immediate cause of Catherine's first mental illness is Edgar's attempt to force her to choose between himself and Heathcliff:

> "I absolutely *require* to know which you choose."
>
> "I require to be let alone!" exclaimed Catherine, furiously. "I demand it! Don't you see I can scarcely stand? Edgar, you—you leave me!" (156)

Catherine, no longer able to put her needs into words, can no longer make herself understood.

The result is a hysterical fit identical to those described by Charcot and made famous by Freud later in the century:

> There she lay dashing her head against the arm of the sofa, and grinding her teeth, so that you might fancy she would crash them to splinters! . . . In a few seconds she stretched herself out stiff, and turned up her eyes, while her cheeks, at once blanched and livid, assumed the aspect of death. (156–57)

The arched back and turned up eyes are classic hysterical symptoms.[3] Hysteria, says Freud, is a translation of repressed desires into body language: that which cannot be put into words is expressed as gestures and physical ailments (*SF*, 97–111). Despite the blood on Catherine's lip, Nelly thinks that nothing serious is wrong because Catherine has planned the fit of passion (156). Nelly suspects that Catherine is putting on a show; she does not understand that hysteria can be both deliberate and genuine. Nelly's reaction to what she calls Catherine's "senseless, wicked rages" is described by Irigaray:

> Artifice, lie, deception, snare—these are the kinds of judgements society confers upon the tableaux, the scenes, the dramas, the pantomimes produced by the hysteric. And if woman's instincts try to command public recognition in this way, their demand and de-monstration will be met with derision, anathema, and punishment. Or at least by belittling interpretations, appeals to common sense or to reason. (*SW*, 125)[4]

While Catherine stays in her room for three days without food, Edgar, as we've seen, spends "his time in the library." Catherine's incredulity—"What in the name of all that feels, has he to do with *books,* when I am dying?" (160)—suggests that she sees in Edgar's books the cause of her frustrations. We have seen that Catherine's diary articulates the desires that are repressed by conventional culture and its ideas of appropriate femininity. It is this very norm which Edgar has accused his wife of transgressing when he questions her morality. By staying locked in his library with his books, Edgar figuratively remains within the dominant ideology, while Catherine strives for the margins.

Unable, in her distracted state of mind, to write her diary, Catherine tries instead to gain the space in which she feels free:

> I wish I were out of doors—I wish I were a girl again, half savage and hardy, and free. . . . I'm sure I should be myself were I once among the heather on those hills. . . . Open the window again wide, fasten it open! Quick, why don't you move? (163)

"Because I won't give you your death of cold," Nelly replies. "You won't give me a chance of life, you mean," retorts Catherine (163). The desires that Catherine has supressed during her marriage to Edgar—chiefly a longing for liberty—surface during her climactic illness in the form of nostalgia for her childhood, and above all a need to be on the heath. As we discussed in the introduction, the heath seems so appropriate for Catherine and Heathcliff because it embodies the liminality which they seek.

Catherine is unable to reach the moors, but she nevertheless retrieves her margin, and recreates a space in which she can articulate what has been repressed. When Catherine tears open her pillow with her teeth, and scatters the feathers everywhere, Nelly observes that the "down is flying about like snow!" (161), thus connecting the scene to the opening of the novel in which Lockwood is lost in a "billowy, white ocean," as a result of wandering into the margins of Catherine's diary (72).

It seems that critics agree with Nelly that Catherine's reveries in this scene are "baby-work" (160). Almost all critics (with the exception of Stevie Davies) avoid Catherine's speech, although I see it as one of the key scenes in the novel, uniting some of the book's major themes and images. Like Ophelia's "mad" speeches in *Hamlet,* Catherine's "nothing" is "more than madness."[5] Catherine's recollection of the lapwings' plundered nest is one of the nest images in the novel which serve to expose the victimization of the women. Catherine's nest represents the effects of Heathcliff's cruelty:

> She seemed to find childish diversion in pulling the feathers from the rents she had just made, and ranging them on the sheet according to their different species: her mind had strayed to other associations.
>
> "That's a turkey's," she murmured to herself; "and this is a wild duck's; and this is a pigeon's. Ah, they put pigeons' feathers in the pillows—no wonder I couldn't die! Let me take care to throw it on the floor when I lie down. And here's a moor-cock's; and this— I should know it among a thousand—it's a lapwing's. Bonny bird; wheeling over our heads in the middle of the moor. It wanted to get to its nest, for the clouds touched the swells, and it felt rain coming. This feather was picked from the heath, the bird was not shot—we saw its nest in the winter, full of little skeletons. Heathcliff set a trap over it, and the old ones dare not come. I made him promise he'd never shoot a lapwing after that, and he didn't. Yes, here are more! Did he shoot my lapwings, Nelly? Are they red, any of them? Let me look." (160)

Catherine clearly identifies with the birds—she calls them "my lapwings"—in their desire to return to the nest because they feel a storm coming. The lapwing, Brontë knew from Thomas Bewick's *History of British Birds* (which the family owned), builds its nest on the open moor: a space at once free and dangerous. The bird "wheeling over our heads in the middle of the moor" is an image of Catherine's longing for freedom and transcendence; but it is shattered by what follows.

Heathcliff had set a trap over the nest, so that the parent birds could not return, and the fledglings inside starved to death. Heathcliff's gratuitous cruelty deprives the nest (the archetypal feminine image) of life. In her reverie Catherine identifies with both the parent and the trapped birds: we later discover that she is very pregnant at this time. She feels trapped by the actions of Heathcliff and Edgar, prevented from inhabiting the moors and all that they represent. Catherine wants, like the lapwing, to soar into space, owned by no one. But Heathcliff, whom she thought understood her needs, has let her down. She does not now trust that he has kept his promise never to kill any more lapwings. The image of the skeletons in the lapwings' nest thus combines Catherine's desire for freedom with her recognition that the men have prevented it. Heathcliff as well as Edgar have trapped her, have sapped her vitality. The nest reverie is therefore central to our understanding of Catherine, as well as being a turning point in the novel. Catherine is dying; Heathcliff and Edgar have plundered the nest.

This neglected scene, then, is not only the culmination of Catherine's life-long conflict, but also embraces many themes that we have traced throughout *Wuthering Heights*. Catherine tears open her pillow and covers her room in feathers, thus creating a white space just like the margins of the tomes in which she wrote her diary. No longer able to write, Catherine nevertheless makes a space in which she can articulate her desires. The meditation on the nest deprived of life represents Catherine's intuitive recognition of her own despoiled femininity. The reverie of the nest full of skeletons is an emblem of herself as object of exchange, as text, trapped by a patriarchal society which demands that she choose whose property she will be. Irigaray claims that "women's bodies—through their use, consumption, and circulation—provide for the condition making social life and culture possible" (*TS,* 171). Catherine recognizes at the end of her life that marriage—being "Mrs. Linton, the lady of Thrushcross Grange,"—was equivalent to being "the wife of a stranger; an exile, and outcast, thenceforth, from what had been my world—You may fancy a glimpse of the abyss where I grovelled" (163). In retrospect then, Catherine calls the respectability of middle-class femininity an "abyss" in which she "grovelled."

Catherine's resistance to being owned through marriage results in starving herself out of existence. She becomes instead consumed by her own mind, and (like Heathcliff when he wishes to die) she refuses external nourishment. Catherine accuses Edgar of wanting only her body, which she says he can have, since she herself far exceeds its constraints:

> "What you touch at present you may have; but my soul will be on that hill-top before you lay hands on me again. I don't want you, Edgar; I'm past wanting you. . . . Return to your books . . . I'm glad you possess a consolation, for all you had in me is gone." (165–66)

Catherine's conviction that she cannot be contained by society's or the men's expectations of her is expressed in the language of transcendence: "I shall be incomparably beyond and above you all"(197); her spirit will not be suppressed:

> "The thing that irks me most is this shattered prison, after all. I'm tired, tired of being enclosed here. I'm wearying to escape into that glorious world . . . not . . . yearning for it through the walls of an aching heart." (196)

Death means escaping from the body that the men wish to own, as a sign of their victory.

Catherine resists being a badge of the men's masculinity: in her youth she disdained femininity, and in her maturity she bitterly protested being an object in the sexual power struggle between Heathcliff and Edgar. Catherine's disappointment with Heathcliff, despite her love for him, is expressed in their final scene: "That is not *my* Heathcliff. I shall love mine yet; and take him with me—he's in my soul" (196). Catherine had believed that Heathcliff, of all the others in her life, was capable of ranging in the margins, but she was mistaken. He, as much as Nelly, had "played traitor," had set a trap over the nest that should have remained indistinguishable from the open moor (166).

Images of margins pervade the representation of Catherine's illness. She longs to be thrown out of heaven onto the heath and she threatens to throw herself out of the window (166), saying that the moors are where she belongs. Peter Miles has commented that Catherine's (along with Frances's) death in childbirth is "a pointed reflection upon woman as a front-line physical victim of human sexuality" (*PM*, 39). But the physical and emotional effects of Catherine's victimization began long before, and are much more complex than, her dying in childbirth. The scene in which Catherine recalls the lapwing's nest is a counterpart not only to her diary, but also to the scenes at the beginning and end of the novel in which her ghost makes its appearance. The ghost, the diary, and the lapwings' nest share a common symbolism: that of the articulation of denied and negated femininity. Catherine's physical existence may be curtailed, but in spite of the sarcasm of Heathcliff's comment to Lockwood, it is true that "her spirit . . . guards the fortunes of Wuthering Heights, even when her body is gone" (55).

9

Megalomania:
The Second Generation and Heathcliff's
Repetition Compulsion

The movie versions of *Wuthering Heights,* apparently for the sake of good drama, ignore the second half of the novel altogether. Most critics agree that the latter part of the novel dealing with the second generation—Cathy, Linton, and Hareton— is weaker than the former. Bersani argues that

> Brontë finally coerces her literary fantasy into a form tame enough
> to satisfy Nelly Dean, and moral enough to put an end to Nelly's . . .
> scolding. (*LB,* 200)

Moser is much more virulent in attacking the second half of *Wuthering Heights* as "simply a superficial stereotyped tale of feminine longings": the story of Cathy and Hareton belongs, he says, "with countless pieces of sub-literary fiction in women's magazines" (*TM,* 15). Everyone at the Heights, he adds, "suffers feminization" at Cathy's hands. While I agree that Cathy effects a "feminization" of the Heights, I do not find this cause for lament, and neither do I find the novel either tamed or turned into pulp romance as a consequence. On the contrary, I hope to demonstrate that the second half of the novel intensifies elements of the first half: we see more overt symbolism of space, more conspicuous male fear of femininity, an escalation in violence, and an explicit link between sexuality and textuality. In the second generation of *Wuthering Heights* the gender and power struggles of the first are writ large. If we, like the movies, ignore the second half of the novel, we miss a crucial part of its message. The second half makes it impossible to regard *Wuthering Heights* as a love story.

We have seen how, in the first part of the novel, geographical location represents the characters' psychological or physical characteristics. Domestic space and the nest are the domains of femininity. The second half of the novel shows how domestic space is used to control women: Cathy is kept within the bounds of Thrushcross Grange by Edgar, until she trespasses onto Heathcliff's land and is then locked up by him. When the reader is first introduced to Cathy she tells Lockwood that "they wouldn't let me go to the end of the garden-wall" (58). Having been forced to marry Linton, Cathy remains imprisoned at Wuthering Heights. Incarceration is Cathy's lot both at the Grange and at the Heights, until Heathcliff's death enables her for the first time to move at liberty.

Cathy is controlled by Edgar and Heathcliff as a consequence of their continued rivalry; she inherits her mother's role in the struggle between the men. The men's fear of feminine sexuality, and the accompanying attempt to turn the woman into a text signifying masculine power, is exhibited in the second generation by Hareton who inherits Heathcliff's misogyny and illiteracy. But Cathy teaches Hareton to read, and, more importantly, to "read" her differently from the way her mother was "read."

The violence in the latter part of the novel escalates as Heathcliff doubles his efforts at revenge. He becomes megalomanic in his desire to possess not only all of the property but also all of the offspring of his enemies. In this part of the novel, Heathcliff attempts to become a species of puppeteer, controlling the lives of others. His appropriation of Hareton, Linton, and Cathy can be seen to be motivated by what Freud calls "a compulsion to repeat." Freud gave this name to the uncontrollable desire on the part of an individual to repeat past "unpleasurable experiences." Repetition compulsion is the mind's attempt to prepare itself retroactively, as it were, for what had been traumatic because beyond control (*SF*, 604–5, 611). In forcing Cathy to marry Linton, and attempting to make them hate each other, Heathcliff somehow hopes to gain control of the past and to make Catherine hate Edgar.

The Cathy-Linton-Hareton triangle is a parody of Catherine-Edgar-Heathcliff. By exaggerating the parents' relations it reveals the absurd though no less tragic consequences of the men's power struggles. The parody in the second half of the novel also has other, more positive, effects; we shall see in the next chapter that Cathy mimics her mother's actions and thereby manages to subvert the homosocial order which victimizes the women.

HEATHCLIFF'S REPETITION COMPULSION

Heathcliff retains the reader's sympathy, Kettle argues, because his revenge has the justice of giving his oppressors a taste of their own medicine (*AK*, 140). Although it is true that Heathcliff employs for revenge "the classic methods of the ruling class, expropriation and property deals," I have already argued that the women are as much a focus of his "expropriation" as are the houses. It is not necessary, after all, as Kavanagh has pointed out, for Cathy to marry Linton in order for Heathcliff to gain control of the property. Linton stands to inherit Thrushcross Grange anyway: "Old Linton's will had stipulated the following order of inheritance: Edgar, then his sons, then Isabella, then her sons" (*JK*, 76). Heathcliff's reasons for "stealing" Linton and Cathy, and forcing them to marry, clearly go beyond his desire to own Thrushcross Grange and Wuthering Heights. Heathcliff maintains his rivalry with, and hatred for, Edgar and Hindley through their children.

Clearly, the deaths of Heathcliff's rivals do not satisfy his desire for revenge. Hindley's death follows from a fight with Heathcliff which appears to be a consummation of the earlier one with Edgar. Although it is much more bloody and brutal, it too is redolent of homosocial and even homoerotic desire. Isabella tells Nelly that the "last glimpse" she had of Heathcliff

> "was a furious rush on his part, checked by an embrace of his host; and both fell locked together on the hearth." (217)

Like his sister Catherine, Hindley loses consciousness embracing Heathcliff. Joseph suspects murder: "He warn't deead when Aw left, nowt uh t'soart!" (222). Edgar's death similarly implicates Heathcliff by occuring just after Heathcliff steals Cathy. Wiping out his rivals does not answer Heathcliff's needs because it also removes the source of his superiority; he must have someone to reflect and affirm his masculine power. Heathcliff appropriates Cathy, Linton, and Hareton in an attempt to seal his victory.

Heathcliff and Edgar displace their "desire" from Catherine to her daughter Cathy, enacting a much more obvious version of their conflicts than in the first part of the novel. Cathy clearly takes the place of her mother in Edgar's affections. She is the Catherine that he had wanted: not only does she look like her mother, but she is similarly high-spirited, imperious with the servants, and "saucy" (224). The important difference, however, is that her love is "never fierce," but "tender" (224)—less extreme, and so less threatening, than her mother's. However, Edgar is taking no chances with this Cathy: she is not told of Heathcliff's existence, and, because of his proximity, is not allowed beyond the grounds of the Grange. Until the age of thirteen she is "a perfect recluse"; and "*apparently* perfectly contented" (225) (my emphasis), just as her mother had seemed with Edgar (139). Although Cathy's enforced seclusion is ostensibly for her own safety, it is clear that by keeping her within bounds Edgar also hopes to curb her mother's spirit in her. Nelly is charged with keeping Cathy at the Grange: her policing role is much more literal and explicit than it had been with Catherine. Although Nelly claims that she "did not fear" Cathy "breaking bounds, because the gates were generally locked, and I thought she would scarcely venture forth alone, if they had stood wide open," Cathy one day jumps her horse over a low part of the hedge and gallops "out of sight" (227). Her ensuing symbolic sexual awakening will be discussed in the next chapter; at present what is significant is that for both Edgar and Heathcliff, control of Cathy parallels jurisdiction over their property. Once Cathy strays beyond bounds, onto the Heights property, she is abducted by Heathcliff, as though her trespass gives him the right to own her (247).

Dragging Cathy and Nelly into Wuthering Heights (248), Heathcliff declares that his "design" is to make the cousins "fall in love, and get married. . . . I desire their union, and am resolved to bring it about" (249). When Heathcliff later locks Cathy in at the Heights, she pleads that her father will be miserable. Heathcliff responds that she could have "hit on no surer way" of remaining where she is: "I shall enjoy myself remarkably in thinking your father will be miserable; I shall not sleep for satisfaction" (306). Heathcliff's intentions in stealing Cathy and forcing her to marry his son are thus directed at Edgar. Heathcliff hopes to make Cathy and Linton hate one another in an attempt to somehow retroactively make Catherine and Edgar hate one another. Cathy unwittingly uncovers the motivation behind Heathcliff's repetition compulsion: "Though you have done what you could to make him hateful to me, and me to him, you *cannot* make us hate each other!" (318). Heathcliff's violent treatment of Cathy is a manifestation of the anger he felt towards Catherine. The shockingly brutal treatment of Cathy brings to the surface Heathcliff's formerly hidden desire to dominate and control her mother.

If Cathy is a repetition of her mother, Linton is a parody of Edgar, as Nelly observes when she first meets him:

A pale, delicate, effeminate boy, who might have been taken for my master's younger brother, so strong was the resemblance; but there was a sickly peevishness in his aspect, that Edgar Linton never had. (235)

Whether it is Linton's "peevishness"—an exaggeration of Edgar's petulance—which incites Heathcliff's violence, or his resemblance to Edgar, he is more cruelly treated than any other male in the novel. Indeed, the treatment of Linton generally in *Wuthering Heights* is so harsh that it almost seems as if the author herself wishes to punish him. The image that the reader retains of Linton is him grovelling at Heathcliff's feet on the moors (300). As a child whose mother has just died, Linton is shunted off, with almost no objection on Edgar's part, to the alien and hostile environment of the Heights. Having lied that the visit would be short (240), Nelly delivers Linton into the hands of an aggressive and malicious parent:

> I bid the trembling child get down, and enter . . . he was not yet certain that the grim, sneering stranger was his father; but he clung to me with growing trepidation . . . (242)

Edgar gives up Linton either to prevent the cold war with the Heights from becoming open hostility, or simply because he's afraid of Heathcliff (237). Linton is an object of exchange (just like his mother before him) between Edgar and Heathcliff, preserving the homosocial relations between them. It is appropriate, then, that Linton assumes a feminine role at the Heights. When he is first taken there, Joseph observes that Edgar must have "swopped wi'ye, maister, an yon's his lass!" (242). Hareton also calls him "more a lass than a lad" (254). Ironically, Linton conforms more closely than any of the women characters to the Victorian ideal of femininity, especially to its cult of invalidism. He is always ill, and either in bed or by the fire, wrappped in a fur cloak, eating "dainties" and drinking milk, complaining alike about Joseph's pipe and about the open window (245). Zillah calls him the most "faint-hearted creature" she has ever known (245). Although Heathcliff loathes his biological son—the "whey-faced whining wretch"—he educates him and preserves his life in hopes of seeing him "fairly lord" of Edgar's estates (243).

Perhaps it is Linton's extreme effeminacy which provokes Heathcliff's most chilling treatment. Heathcliff does not merely mark Linton as his own, with the violence that he exhibits towards the women, but he succeeds in making Linton a puppet whose every action is determined by himself. The torture that achieves this, however, is not explicit, which leaves the reader to imagine (with his or her own terrors) what happens before the "afterwards":

> "You'll see by his look that he has recieved his due! I brought him down one evening, the day before yesterday, and just set him in a chair, and never touched him afterwards. I sent Hareton out, and we

had the room to ourselves. In two hours, I called Joseph to carry him up again; and, since then, my presence is as potent on his nerves, as a ghost; and I fancy he sees me often, though I am not near. Hareton says he wakes and shrieks in the night by the hour together." (318)

Heathcliff imprints himself on Linton's "nerves." Although he inscribes Catherine, Isabella, and Cathy with visible marks of ownership, he prefers psychological means to coerce the men. Nelly wonders how it is that Heathcliff's every move produces, in Linton, profound terror:

Linton had sunk prostrate again in another paroxysm of helpless fear, caused by his father's glance towards him, I suppose; there was nothing else to produce such humiliation. He made several efforts to obey, but his little strength was annihilated, for the time, and he fell back again with a moan. (300)

In this scene on the moor, Linton is Heathcliff's puppet, devoid of his own will; even physically, he resembles a rag-doll whom Heathcliff props against "a ridge of turf," and holds up himself (300). Linton's abjection serves to underline Heathcliff's brutalities to the women. Heathcliff's violence in the second half of the novel thus reaches grotesque proportions. By reiterating that his victims are his "own"— he says of Hareton for example, "I've got him faster than his scoundrel of a father secured me, and lower" (253)—Heathcliff reveals that he is motivated by a desire to make his victims his property.

Although Hareton apparently is not subjected to violence, he too receives Heathcliff's psychological imprint. Nelly observes that although Heathcliff had not treated Hareton "physically ill" he had

bent his malevolence on making him a brute: he was never taught to read or write; never rebuked for any bad habit which did not annoy his keeper; never led a single step towards virtue, or guarded by a single precept against vice. (231)

Hareton is the only character in the novel for whom Heathcliff feels empathy, perhaps as a result of having fashioned Hareton in his own image:

"I can sympathise with all his feelings, having felt them myself—
I know what he suffers now, for instance, exactly. . . . And he'll
never be able to emerge from his bathos of coarseness, and igno-
rance. I've got him faster than his scoundrel of a father secured me,
and lower; for he takes a pride in his brutishness. I've taught him to
scorn everything extra-animal as silly and weak." (252–53)

Heathcliff's aim to produce surrogates, and to repeat the past, is so
successful that he cannot finally complete his plan of revenge. Just
when Hareton, courting Cathy, seems to be "a personification of"
Heathcliff's own "youth," Heathcliff discovers that he has "lost the
faculty of enjoying" his enemies' destruction (353). In a lengthy self-
reflection which is worth quoting in full, Heathcliff recognizes not
only the irony of his situation, but the role of his "representatives" in
his need to repeat:

"It is a poor conclusion, is it not. . . . An absurd termination to my
violent exertions? . . . [W]hen everything is ready, and in my power,
I find the will to lift a slate off either roof has vanished! My old enemies have not beaten me—now would be the precise time to revenge
myself on their representatives—I could do it; and none could hin-
der me—But where is the use? I don't care for striking, I can't take
the trouble to raise my hand! That sounds as if I had been labouring
the whole time, only to exhibit a fine trait of magnanimity. It is far
from being the case—I have lost the faculty of enjoying their destruction, and I am too idle to destroy for nothing." (353)

It is not remorse, says Heathcliff, that has diverted his search for
revenge. He is, rather, "devoured" (354) by a different (although I
argue interrelated) desire—"My soul's bliss kills my body, but does
not satisfy itself" (363)—the desire for Catherine.

Heathcliff tells Nelly, with no apparent awareness of perversion,
that he has twice exhumed Catherine's body, and has at last found
relief in her "passionless features" (320). Catherine's "passionless"
features show her to be devoid of her own will. By denying to himself
that she is dead—"I'll have her in my arms again! If she be cold, I'll
think it is this north wind that chills me; and if she be motionless, it is
sleep" (320)—Heathcliff can have his fantasy of complete control.

The second time he exhumes Catherine's grave, it is eighteen years later, just after Edgar's death, and Heathcliff is still motivated by rivalry:

> "I'll tell you what I did yesterday! I got the sexton, who was digging Linton's grave, to remove the earth off her coffin lid, and I opened it. I thought, once, I would have stayed there, when I saw her face again—it is hers yet—he had hard work to stir me; but he said it would change, if the air blew on it, and so I struck one side of the coffin loose—and covered it up—not Linton's side, damn him! I wish he'd been soldered in lead—and I bribed the sexton to pull it away, when I'm laid there, and slide mine out too. I'll have it made so, and then, by the time Linton gets to us, he'll not know which is which!" (319)

Heathcliff's desire for fusion in the grave with Catherine—a kind of sexual intercourse through decay—represents the ultimate triumph over Edgar. All his life Heathcliff has marked women in an effort to turn them into texts of his potency and power; what better than a dead woman to confirm his control? It is Catherine's corpse, he admits, which finally pacifies him: "unless I had received a distinct impression of her passionless features, that strange feeling would hardly have been removed" (320). Catherine's dead body, which Heathcliff claims is unaltered in eighteen years, "consoles" (321) him more than forcing Cathy to marry Linton, more than turning Hareton into a brute, and Linton into a rag-doll. Heathcliff even believes that Catherine's body will not begin to change and decay without him: "I'm better pleased that it should not commence till I share it" (320).

In Catherine's "passionless features" Heathcliff finds what he had been seeking:

> "A sudden sense of relief flowed, from my heart, through every limb. I relinquished my labour of agony, and turned consoled at once, unspeakably consoled." (321)

At last the woman is truly a text, a totally will-less and empty reflection of Heathcliff's authority.

Like Catherine, Heathcliff is extremely candid as he leads up to his similarly self-willed death. He himself admits to "frenzy" and "compulsion" in all his actions (354). But the compulsion to repeat the past is turned, by virtue of Catherine's corpse, into a desire to escape his body, as she did, through death:

> "It is by compulsion, that I do the slightest act, not prompted by one thought, and by compulsion, that I notice anything alive or dead, which is not associated with one universal idea . . . I have a single wish, and my whole being and faculties are yearning to attain it. They have yearned towards it so long, and so unwaveringly, that I'm convinced it *will* be reached—and *soon*—because it has devoured my existence—I am swallowed in the anticipation of its fulfilment." (354)

In other words, Heathcliff has no thoughts, no purpose; he is simply devoured by desire.

When Nelly finds Heathcliff dead he has apparently re-enacted, in order to reverse, Lockwood's encounter with Catherine's ghost:

> The bed-clothes dripped, and he was perfectly still. The lattice, flapping to and fro, had grazed one hand that rested on the sill—no blood trickled from the broken skin, and when I put my fingers to it, I could doubt no more—he was dead and stark! (364–65)

The scene uncannily repeats Lockwood's famous nightmare. All the ingredients are recognizable but different: the dripping bed-clothes (this time with rain); the open or broken lattice or casement; and the cut (but this time bloodless) hand. Unlike Lockwood, who would not admit Catherine's ghost, Heathcliff dies in the attempt.

The second generation of *Wuthering Heights,* far from being a pale imitation of the first, as many critics claim, intensifies the conflicts of the first generation. Perhaps it is because it exaggerates, almost to absurdity, the sexual and affective relations that critics such as Moser find it hard to swallow what had been only implied in the first half.[1] Linton and Hareton are caricatures of Edgar and Heathcliff, while Cathy perpetuates her mother's rebellious spirit. In lamenting that Cathy's marriage to Linton is tantamount to tying "herself to a perishing little monkey" (304), Nelly hints at its role as a parody of Catherine's marriage to Edgar. Cathy's marriages reverse the order of her mother's names on the window-sill (61): she moves from Linton to Heathcliff to Earnshaw, so that the generations come full circle. Bersani comments that "The claustrophobic inbreeding in the novel is paralleled by psychological repetitions which also draw the characters into a single family" (*LB*, 199). The closed circle of family relations makes it seem that there is no escape from the partriarchal and homosocial order that has such devastating effects on the women, but we shall see in the following chapter that Cathy does disrupt the cycle of repetition and challenge Heathcliff's compulsion to repeat the conflicts and abuses of the first generation.

10

The "Property" Changes Hands: Cathy's Challenge to Patriarchy

As a prelude to the final conflicts at the Heights we see Hareton "hanging a litter of puppies from a chairback in the doorway" (217). In light of the connection we've seen between dogs and women in *Wuthering Heights* this prepares us for what follows. Cathy is (as we saw in chapter 7) horrendously maltreated at the Heights: Heathcliff batters her frequently (302, 313), instructing his son to do the same (305), and symbolically rapes her (313). Heathcliff beats Cathy because she resists him (although he had beaten Isabella because she didn't [188]). Having slapped Cathy's head several times, Heathcliff warns:

> "You shall have plenty of that—you can bear plenty—you're no weakling—you shall have a daily taste, if I catch such a devil of a temper in your eyes again!" (303)

Cathy is, however, more successful than her mother at challenging Heathcliff's domination. She does, as Moser says, "feminize" the Heights (*TM*, 15)—by creating her own space for feminine inscription, and by teaching Hareton, the remaining representative of the homosocial order, to read texts (and women) differently. By seducing Hareton into a feminine domain, Cathy intervenes in the homosocial relations that have dominated the novel.

Heathcliff is proud of his "coarse" and "ignorant . . . son" Hareton, in whom he fosters both illiteracy and misogyny (252–53). Heathcliff teaches Hareton, as much by example as by precept, to see women and books alike as threats. Heathcliff prevents his victims and his surrogates from reading: "Mr. Heathcliff never reads," Cathy tells Lockwood, "so he took it into his head to destroy my books" (332); this "vicious act," says Van de Laar, reveals Heathcliff's "impotent frustration at being unable to subdue [Cathy's] independent spirit" (*VL*, 203). Cathy, unlike her mother, has "no materials for writing, not even a book from which I might tear a leaf" (331). When Heathcliff sees her reading he commands: "Put your trash away, and find something to do . . . do you hear, damnable jade?" (72). "Trash," is also a term for women who are sexually transgressive, and "jade" is another name for a "whore"—Heathcliff's words betray that the threat posed by a woman to his masculinity increases with her access to reading and writing. We shall see that Cathy exploits the sexual nature of the activity.

Van de Laar observes that "Cathy must not be allowed to seek (through her books) a way out of the living death" that Heathcliff has imposed upon her (*VL*, 205). Yet, while still in the relative safety of Thrushcross Grange, Cathy's reading and writing are restricted (262). Writing letters to Linton is forbidden to her not only because Linton is the recipient, but also, it seems, because the activity itself is taboo. Nelly had seen Cathy

> Standing at the table with a bit of blank paper before her, and a pencil in her hand, which she guiltily slipped out of sight, on my re-entrance. (257)

If the letters were merely childish "trash," as Nelly claims, she would not need to subject them to "immolation" (261), or ritual burning. The significance of Cathy's letter writing is further emphasized by the imagery in which her hoard of epistles is presented. This is the last of the three images in the novel of a plundered nest representing femininity. Nelly unlocks Cathy's cabinet drawer, and removes her secret "treasures." Cathy returns to find it empty:

> Never did any bird flying back to a plundered nest which it had left brim-full of chirping young ones, express more complete despair in its anguished cries and flutterings, than she by her single 'Oh!' and the change that transfixed her late happy countenance. (259)

Cathy's letter writing means as much to her as the diary had to her mother: both are expressions of active desire, and as such are viewed by others as transgressive of Victorian norms of passive femininity. In being despoiled of her "mysterious treasures," Cathy is deprived of her creativity (258). If Nelly means what she says in comparing Cathy's despair to that of a mother bird finding an empty nest, then her subsequent actions are incredibly cruel: she forces Cathy to witness the burning of her literary offspring (260–61). Reading and writing for Catherine and Cathy alike are intimately bound up with their feminine desires. Although Heathcliff tries to prevent such expressions at the Heights, Cathy finds a way around it.

It is not far off the mark to argue that it is Hareton who introduces Cathy to the "mysterious treasures" of her awakening sexual desire which finds its first outlet in her letters to Linton. Until the age of thirteen, Cathy had never been beyond the walls of Thrushcross Grange. When she reaches adolescence, however, she longs to visit "Penistone Crags" (the phallic suggestion is unavoidable), and she one day breaks out of the grounds in order to do so (226–27). Hareton subsequently "opened the mysteries of the fairy cave" to her (233).

Cathy and Hareton's introduction to each other echoes Catherine and Heathcliff in their adolescence. When Cathy visits the Heights she is subjected to a "canine attack" just like her mother at the same age (which we've seen is a sexual initiation). Cathy then visits the famous "fairy cave" at "Penistone Crags" with Hareton (232–33). But when she afterwards treats him as a servant, he "damns" her and calls her a "saucy witch" (230). Cathy is horrified to discover that Hareton is her cousin: "Pausing in her lamentations, she surveyed him with a glance of awe and horror, then burst forth anew" (231). This is an exaggerated echo of Catherine's dismay, after her assimilation into "respectable" femininity, with Heathcliff's "rude" breeding and dirtiness. Like Heathcliff at the same age, Hareton is "attired in garments befitting his daily occupations of working on the farm, and lounging among the moors after rabbits and game" (231). Also like Heathcliff (and Lockwood), Hareton is extremely discomfited by a woman's gaze: "He could not stand a steady gaze" from Cathy's eyes (229). Heathcliff advises Hareton how to act with Cathy:

> "And behave like a gentleman, mind! Don't use any bad words; and don't stare, when the young lady is not looking at you, and be ready to hide your face when she is; and when you speak, say your words slowly, and keep your hands out of your pockets." (252)

Newman argues that preventing Hareton from looking and being looked at effectively prevents a sense of self: "Heathcliff has carefully cultivated Hareton's degradation by cutting the boy off from the specular relations in which subjectivity is constituted" (*BN*, 1036). But it is specifically the woman's gaze, as Newman herself points out, that Hareton fears: "Heathcliff is teaching Hareton to fear the female gaze and to associate it with imposed muteness" (*BN*, 1036). Heathcliff's fear of the female gaze, as we saw in chapter 7, issues in violence. So long as he continues to follow Heathcliff's example, Hareton is complicit in the abuse of Cathy; he turns a blind eye to her being brutalized at the Heights. So long as Cathy submits to Heathcliff's battering, Linton's cowardly abuse, Hareton's anger, and Joseph's scorn, she (unwillingly) upholds masculine domination and homosocial relations. The bonds between the men—especially between Heathcliff and Hareton and Joseph and Hareton—continue at Cathy's expense.

But Cathy challenges Heathcliff's domination with more than her gaze: she perpetuates, with greater success, her mother's subversive activity of writing back to the dominant male discourse. She does so not only with her mother's practice of inscribing a feminine space in a male domain, but also by actively mimicking the position in which patriarchy, and its homosocial relations, places women. Cathy uses parody and mimicry to undermine a social order which depends on debasing women to the function of signs. We have seen in the first half of the novel that Heathcliff, Lockwood, and Edgar see women as objects, which through exchange, ensure ties between the men. In a social order dominated by men, the women are signs of an agreement to maintain that order. We have also seen that Heathcliff literalizes the woman's role as a document of masculine domination: he beats and metaphorically rapes Cathy to signify that she is his property (chap. 7). The bruises and cuts on the women bear witness to Heathcliff's victory over other men. At first Cathy is forced into this role—she is more brutalized than any other character in the novel—but she resists by recognizing and making clear that she is performing as a text. By parodying the role of woman as a sign in patriarchal society, Cathy makes explicit what must be hidden in order to function.

The courtship between Cathy and Hareton, critics have noted, is "a battle of the books," which revolves around reading (VL, 206). However, in view of Catherine's diary and Cathy's letters as subversive inscriptions of feminine desire, reading and writing have implications far beyond simply that of literacy. In teaching Hareton to read, Cathy, as Moser laments, also feminizes him.

Heathcliff almost succeeds in turning Cathy into a ghost like her mother. After spending weeks at Linton's death-bed, Cathy says "You have left me so long to struggle against death, alone, that I feel and see only death! I feel like death!" Zillah remarks "And she looked like it, too!" (325). Just as she is almost reduced to the "zero" that Joseph and Heathcliff would like—"I've been starved a month and more" (327), she says, meaning that she's been frozen to death—Cathy spies some books. It is as if the books give her life:

> Having sat till she was warm, she began to look round, and discovered a number of books in the dresser; she was instantly upon her feet again, stretching to reach them. (327)

Hareton helps her to fill her frock—"a great advance for the lad"—and

> ventured to stand behind as she examined them, and even to stoop
> and point out what struck his fancy in certain old pictures which
> they contained—nor was he daunted by the saucy style in which she
> jerked the page from his finger; he contented himself with going a
> bit farther back, and looking at her instead of the book. (327)

When Cathy will not allow Hareton to touch the book, he switches
from gazing at it to gazing at her. The identification between Cathy
and her book is even more explicit in what follows:

> At last, he proceeded from staring to touching; he put out his hand
> and stroked one curl, as gently as if it were a bird. He might have
> stuck a knife into her neck, she started round in such a taking. (327)

This unites much of the significant imagery in the novel: Cathy is both
a book and a creature who inhabits a nest. When Hareton tries to
touch, it is as though he has stabbed her (the last injury Heathcliff
inflicted on Isabella was a knife flung at her neck [217]). When Hareton tries to touch Cathy instead of the book, she responds identically
by snatching herself away: " 'Get away, this moment! How dare you
touch me? Why are you stopping there?' she cried in a tone of disgust" (327). The last remark, although ambiguous, suggests that Cathy
expects more—likely the same treatment that she has received from
Heathcliff.

Following this, Hareton seems to recognize that reading and
writing strengthen Cathy's sense of self. He intercepts a letter to
Cathy, "saying Mr. Heathcliff should look at it first" (331). Cathy
describes to Lockwood her efforts to find books at the Heights after
Heathcliff destroyed hers (it is a pity she has not found her mother's
tomes, or she might have "torn a leaf" from them, metaphorically as
well as literally): "I have not had a glimpse of one, for weeks. Only
once, I searched through Joseph's store of theology, to his great irrita-
tion; and once, Hareton, I came upon a secret stock in your room"
(332). The books are so much a part of the people that Joseph is
affronted by Cathy searching through his, and Hareton "blushed crim-
son, when his cousin made this revelation of his private literary
accomplishments" (as though he had been discovered masturbating)

(332). Cathy is again robbed of her "treasures" (just as she had been by Nelly): "perhaps *your* envy counselled Mr. Heathcliff to rob me of my treasures?" she asks Hareton, "But I've most of them written on my brain and printed in my heart, and you cannot deprive me of those!" (332). Recognizing the link between herself and her books, Cathy internalizes them, makes them a part of herself. Like her mother, Cathy engulfs and absorbs her texts.

Cathy demonstrates the link between texts and women much more explicitly than other women characters in *Wuthering Heights*. She refuses those that Hareton has "debased":

> "He has no right to appropriate what is mine, and make it ridiculous to me with his vile mistakes and mispronunciations! Those books, both prose and verse, were consecrated to me by other associations, and I hate to have them debased and profaned in his mouth!" (332–33)

Cathy regards Hareton's misreadings as maltreatment—as the profanation and debasement—of her volumes: "I won't have them, now . . . I shall connect them with you, and hate them" (333). When she imitates Hareton's reading, he hits her and begins to "hurl" the books on the fire: "'Yes, that's all the good that such a brute as you can get from them!' cried Catherine, sucking her damaged lip, and watching the conflagration with indignant eyes" (333–34). For the second time in her life Cathy watches her "treasures" go up in smoke. Like Heathcliff, Hareton vents his anger and frustration on books and women.

Cathy, however, effects a turn of events by exploiting the connection between herself and the books. In a deliberate mimicry of the position in which she is placed by Heathcliff and Hareton, Cathy turns herself into a text, and offers it to Hareton. At first, when she tries to force herself and her books on him, Hareton tells her to "go to the devil!," but Cathy insists "you shall own me" (343); then, "after remaining an instant, undecided, she stooped, and impressed on his cheek a gentle kiss" (344). The kiss is described as an imprint, making it the direct opposite of Heathcliff's violent inscriptions on women's faces. Cathy wraps up a book like a gift, and addresses it to Hareton, promising that if he accept it she shall "teach him to read it *right*"

(345; my emphasis). The point is not simply that he should be able to read, but that he should be able to read in a particular way.

Cathy's actions constitute a sexual overture to Hareton. After the kiss, he at first "remains on the defensive" (*BN*, 1037). Having been taught by Heathcliff to fear Cathy's gaze, Hareton "was very careful, for some minutes, that his face should not be seen; and when he did raise it, he was sadly puzzled where to turn his eyes"(344–45). When Hareton does unwrap the gift he is evidently aroused: "he trembled, and his face glowed" (354). There follows, as Newman points out, a significant gap in the text, after which Cathy and Hareton are as lovers (*BN*, 1037); "I overheard no further distinguishable talk," says Nelly:

> but on looking round again, I perceived two such radiant counte-
> nances bent over the accepted book, that I did not doubt the treaty
> had been ratified, on both sides, and the enemies were, thenceforth,
> sworn allies. (345)

The "treaty," says Newman, represents "the momentous occasion of an exchange of gazes that does not annihilate the male gazer" as the men in the novel fear (*BN*, 1037). Cathy has successfully taught Hareton to read *her* "right."

Cathy's mother Catherine had challenged patriarchal ideology by covering "testaments" and "tomes" with her own counter-testa-ment (62). Catherine's diary creates a feminine space, visually and intellectually, in a masculine domain. Cathy's version of this subver-sive activity is to make a different space, but the effect is very similar, especially on the men. Cathy creates a flower garden in the midst of Joseph's fruit bushes. Zillah is

> terrified at the devastation which had been accomplished in a brief
> half hour; the black currant trees were the apple of Joseph's eye, and
> she had just fixed her choice of a flower bed in the midst of them!
> (347)

Cathy's flower bed is highly significant. Alice Walker, in *In Search of Our Mothers' Gardens,* discusses the importance of a garden as cre-ative expression, as self-realization, to her Black American female ancestors who were denied access to reading and writing. Walker describes her mother's flower garden as: "the Art that is her gift":

> And so our mothers and grandmothers have, more often than not anonymously, handed on the creative spark, the seed of the flower they themselves never hoped to see: or like a sealed letter they could not plainly read.[1]

Cathy's flower bed can be seen similarly as the "sealed letter" she hopes to leave for the next generation of women. It is evident that Heathcliff has been unable to destroy her creative spark, her resistance. Cathy's flower bed, moreover, like her mother's diary, defaces a masculine domain: it literally erodes Joseph's province. Joseph's "bitter injuries" link his devastated fruit garden to the seduction of Hareton.

The other "apple" of Joseph's "eye" is Hareton, whom he covets. Joseph (as we've seen) is extremely upset by Cathy caressing "ahr lad" (449), and he explicitly sexualizes the threat she poses: "This hoile's norther mensful, nor seemly fur us—we mun side aht, and seearch another!" (346). Because Hareton helps Cathy to make her bed (as it were!), Joseph believes she has bewitched him; he "laments" to Heathcliff his "bitter injuries":

> "It's yon flaysome, graceless quean, ut's witched ahr lad, wi' her bold een, un her forrard ways—till—Nay! it fair brusts my heart! He's forgotten all E done for him, un made on him, un' goan un' riven up a whole row ut t' grandest currant trees, i' t' garden!" (349)

Not only does Joseph couple Cathy's flower garden with her seduction of Hareton, he also links both to the threat of her gaze—her "bold een." To Joseph, Cathy's misdemeanors constitute sexual threats. Furthermore, Cathy has disrupted the close relations between the men: Hareton, "our lad," has "forgotten," says Joseph, what Heathcliff has "made on him."

Joseph is described as "unmanned" by Cathy's actions. When we recall that Joseph represents the central, misogynistic values of the society of *Wuthering Heights*, then Cathy is delivering a direct challenge to those values. Heathcliff calls Cathy an "insolent slut," further emphasizing that her rebellion is perceived as a sexual threat and transgression (349). Cathy, just like her mother, fills in the feminine gap in the masculine creative domain, but she is more successful at "unmanning" Hareton, Joseph, and Heathcliff.

Cathy enlists Hareton in her resistance to the homosocial and patriarchal regime of Joseph and Heathcliff: he helps make the flower bed which enrages Joseph, learns to read against Heathcliff's wishes, and discovers the wherewithal to return Cathy's gaze. Finally, he and Cathy find the courage to laugh in Heathcliff's presence, which is perhaps the most rebellious of all their actions. At breakfast on the morning of the devastated fruit garden, Cathy provokes Hareton:

> He dared not speak to her, there; he dared hardly look; and yet she went on teasing, till he was twice on the point of being provoked to laugh; and I frowned, and then she glanced towards the master . . . at last, Hareton uttered a smothered laugh. (348)

Heathcliff assumes that it is Cathy who laughs:

> "What fiend possesses you to stare back at me, continually, with those infernal eyes? Down with them! and don't remind me of your existence again. I thought I had cured you of laughing!" (348)

Hareton admits "It was me," and Heathcliff does nothing. Critics such as Irigaray and Hélène Cixous have explored the subversive nature of laughter. Because it upsets the balance of power, and disarms authority, laughter can be a weapon against oppression (*TS*, 163).[2] The laughter of Cathy and Hareton is a prelude to a shift in the relations at the Heights. When Cathy "recklessly" insists on her rights to the garden, Heathcliff goes to strike her, but she declares: "If you strike me, Hareton will strike you! . . . so you may as well sit down" (350). Heathcliff is outraged: "Damnable witch! dare you pretend to rouse him against me?" (350). Cathy, however, is clear that this is a turning point: "He'll not obey you, wicked man, any more!" (350). It *is* a turning-point. Although he seems "ready to tear Catherine in pieces,"

Heathcliff suddenly relaxes his grip and speaks to Cathy "with assumed calmness." Cathy has "unmanned" him.

Earlier in the novel, laughter had similarly challenged Heathcliff's authoritarianism. Isabella finally escapes his "murderous violence" through derision (209). Witnessing Hindley, after being stabbed and beaten by Heathcliff, kneeling to pray in a pool of his own blood, Isabella laughs; she tells Nelly later that she felt "as reckless as some malefactors show themselves at the foot of the gallows" (214). Though shocking, Isabella's laughter is evidence of the awakening "instinct of self-preservation" (209). She reacts to Heathcliff's apparently intense grief over Catherine with jubilation:

> "I stared full at him, and laughed scornfully. The clouded windows of hell flashed a moment towards me; the fiend which usually looked out, however, was so dimmed and drowned that I did not fear to hazard another sound of derision." (217)

Isabella's scorn diminishes Heathcliff's aggression. After telling Heathcliff that if Catherine had married him she would have "presented a similar picture" to herself, she runs away from the Heights never to return (217).

It is not difficult to see why the early reviewers of the novel were upset by the brutality of *Wuthering Heights*. Perhaps even more shocking than Heathcliff's violence is Isabella, the epitome of respectable Victorian femininity, laughing at it. Laughter is, says Patricia Yaeger, one of the ways in which *Wuthering Heights* is able to "rupture the authoritative, the normative, the social" (*PY*, 195). Using the weapons of mimicry, parody, and laughter, Cathy successfully disrupts Heathcliff's homosocial regime.

11

A (Provisional) Conclusion,
and A Warning About Visual Aids!

Hillis Miller claims that "Even more than some other great works of literature," *Wuthering Heights* "seems to have an inexhaustible power to call forth commentary and more commentary":

> All literary criticism tends to be the presentation of what claims to be the definitive rational explanation of the text in question. (*HM*, 50)

Because I agree with Hillis Miller that almost all of the interpretations of *Wuthering Heights* take the "form of an attempted reasonable formulation of its unreason"—that *Wuthering Heights* is a novel which resists an exhaustive explanation—I shall offer here a provisional conclusion and add a warning about the use of visual aids to interpret this elusive novel.

Most critics, including myself, are perplexed by the conclusion to *Wuthering Heights*. There seem to be two opposing and equally unsatisfying reactions: on the one hand are critics who see the conclusion as humanizing the excesses of the past: "the novel affirms the domesticated virtues of man as a kind and social creature" (*IE*, 128).

In this version, the relationship between Cathy and Hareton represents "an alleviation of suffering and loneliness through love that is kindness, affection . . . in a domestic context" (*IE*, 128). Cathy, unlike her mother, "is able to . . . get a moral education from her sufferings."[1] On the other hand, critics such as Moser cannot take Cathy and Hareton seriously—the "saccharine speeches," and "thin-blooded" characters, reveal that Brontë "writes insincerely" (*TM*, 14, 13). The film adaptations avoid the dilemma by leaving out the second generation entirely.

I do not agree either that Cathy and Hareton represent Brontë's ideal, the solution to the social problems explored in the novel, or that they are entirely ridiculous and therefore without meaning. While Moser is right that there is a great deal that is ironic (though not contemptible) in the conclusion to *Wuthering Heights,* he is, I believe, mistaken in arguing that "there is . . . no evidence that Emily Brontë perceived that irony" (*TM*, 18). While I do not wish to speculate on Brontë's conscious intentions, which can only ever remain at the level of speculation, I would like to draw attention to the fact that it is Lockwood who describes Cathy and Hareton in those passages which seem so insincere (338, 367), and it is Lockwood who offers the closing "moral" to *Wuthering Heights.* And Lockwood was revealed early in the novel as an impotent reader and unreliable interpreter of people and events.

Seeing Cathy teaching Hareton to read, Lockwood admits that: "I bit my lip, in spite, at having thrown away the chance I might have had, of doing something besides staring at [Cathy's] smiting beauty" (338). But we know that Lockwood can only stare. As well as being envious, he is sentimental and unrealistic—throughout the story which Nelly has related to him he has cherished an illusion that Cathy might fall in love with him (55, 191, 288), and now he is confronted by her kissing someone else:

> "Con-*trary*!" said a voice, as sweet as a silver bell—"That for the third time, you dunce! I'm not going to tell you, again—Recollect, or I'll pull your hair!"
> "Contrary, then," answered another, in deep, but softened tones. "And now, kiss me, for minding so well." (338)

Nothing could be further from the mutual recriminations that make up Catherine and Heathcliff's passionate last love scene (197), but both have elements of irony. The irony, perhaps, is that we read love into both the spectacle of Heathcliff "gnash[ing]" and "foam[ing]" like "a mad dog," and into Cathy threatening to pull Hareton's hair if he doesn't pronounce his words correctly.

The relation of Cathy to Hareton at the end of the novel is that of teacher and pupil: Cathy has the dominant position (339). I have argued that Cathy effectively challenges the closed circle of homosocial relations, and that the second half of the novel is therefore crucial in showing how marginalized feminine voices can disrupt the status quo. However, Cathy challenges Heathcliff's tyrannical perpetuation of homosociality through an act of parody or imitation. Recognizing that the threat posed by women reading was that they could not then be blank pages to be marked with a man's imprint, Cathy deliberately parodies a social order which would turn women into texts. Engaging in imitation or "mimesis," says Irigaray,

> [i]s thus, for a woman, to try to recover the place of her exploitation by discourse, without allowing herself to be simply reduced to it. It means to resubmit herself . . . to ideas about herself, that are elaborated in/by a masculine logic, but so as to make "visible," by an effect of playful repetition, what was supposed to remain invisible. (*TS*, 76)

While it is true that Cathy succeeds in exposing or making "visible" that the exchange of women turns them into texts, into signs of masculine domination, we may question the extent of her challenge to patriarchy. Although Cathy takes the sexual initiative with Hareton, and turns the tables by forcing him to "own" her, as she puts it (343), she nevertheless does give herself to him in marriage. At the end of *Wuthering Heights* Hareton Earnshaw, by default, "owns" all the property of the two families, and the surviving women! However, Cathy is no longer an object, nor is she physically, sexually, and mentally abused. That Cathy's challenge to patriarchy is not conclusive is, however, inevitable.

The principal reason, however, for the provisional nature of my conclusion, is that the subversiveness of what I have called "the writing in the margins" in *Wuthering Heights* depends on the reader. Lockwood was afraid to listen to Catherine's ghost, to let her into the center of his vision. My study of *Wuthering Heights* has depended on the reader's willingness to attend to that in the text which is usually ignored, or considered unimportant: Catherine's diary, her death-bed reverie, Cathy's flower garden, and the images of the nest, for example. The most significant marginalized element in *Wuthering Heights,* however, is Catherine's ghost which—as Musselwhite hints (*DM,* 155)—makes it impossible for us to make up our minds about *Wuthering Heights.* At the end of the novel Lockwood is still unable to admit Catherine's ghost into his vision. Despite being told by Nelly that all the local people, including Joseph, believe that Heathcliff and Catherine still "walk," and that she had met a lad crying because "They's Heathcliff, and a woman, yonder, under t'Nab . . . un'Aw darnut pass 'em" (366), Lockwood remains unable to "imagine" such things. Contemplating the graves of Catherine, Edgar, and Heathcliff, Lockwood

> lingered round them, under that benign sky; watched the moths fluttering among the heath and hare-bells; listened to the soft wind breathing through the grass; and wondered how anyone could ever imagine unquiet slumbers, for the sleepers in that quiet earth. (367)

The closing lines of *Wuthering Heights* are clearly ironic, and Lockwood a disappointing surrogate reader.

A WARNING ABOUT VISUAL AIDS

Wuthering Heights is an inconclusive and unsettling novel. Perhaps this is why it seems to elicit critical efforts to "tame" and even subdue it. One manifestation of the desire to rationalize *Wuthering Heights* is the critics' predilection for visual aids. If you are coming to the novel for the first time you may notice that it is almost impossible to find an introductory reading of this work that does not have charts or diagrams. U.C. Knoepflmacher's "Landmarks of World Literature" study, for example, includes the usual Linton-Earnshaw family tree, chronology and internal chronology of *Wuthering Heights*, as well as a diagram of literal and metaphoric brother/sister pairs, and a table of narrative voices other than Nelly's.[2]

The popularity of visual aids to explain *Wuthering Heights* might result from its reliance on spatial images, which encourage visualization. Nevertheless, it is rather surprising that such a novel should elicit so many explanatory charts and diagrams; surprising, because the image of Brontë as an accidental artist and the novel as a sort of natural phenomenon has persisted despite the charts; surprising also, because *Wuthering Heights* remains an enigmatic text.

The conception of *Wuthering Heights* as spontaneous and inartistic predominated until C.P. Sanger's discovery, as we have seen, of a careful and logical structure to what had been considered an emotional outpouring. Sanger demonstrated "a remarkable piece of symmetry in a tempestuous book" (*MA*, 123), by constructing, from the dates given in the novel, a Linton-Earnshaw family tree, showing the births, deaths, and marriages of all the members. Although Sanger performed the service of demonstrating that, far from being a work of accidental genius, *Wuthering Heights* has a thorough internal plan, he initiated an epidemic of charts and diagrams for the novel.

Perhaps it is because *Wuthering Heights* is so disturbing that it elicits diagrams: they seem to be an attempt to impose order, to control and contain the novel. But the diagrams are not only at odds with the spirit of the novel, they frequently distort it. Knoepflmacher's list of narrative segments, for example, in which "the reader, rather than Nelly, is intended to be the prime auditor" is, for the sake of simplicity, extremely misleading (*UK*, 53). Knoepflmacher claims that the sections he quotes elude Nelly's control (*UK*, 55); but if we look at (f) for example, the section in chapter 17 in which Isabella describes running away from Heathcliff, we will see that Isabella's speech is actually at *third* remove from the reader: she tells Nelly, who is telling Lockwood, who is recording it in his diary. Furthermore, when Isabella reports Heathcliff's words, they are at *fourth* remove. Nothing in *Wuthering Heights* escapes the control or biases of either Lockwood or Nelly. The point is that not only is the reader never the prime auditor, as Knoepflmacher's diagram suggests, but that what is called *Wuthering Heights'* narrative imbedding—a story (Nelly's) within a story (Lockwood's)—makes it impossible to distinguish *who* is speaking. The "Chinese box" structure, or "nested" framing of *Wuthering Heights* also produces nested discourse (*VG*, 158; *PM*, 30). Are we *supposed* to disentangle indistinguishable voices? Or is there a point to their superimposition? The reader is simultaneously aligned with Lockwood the detached voyeur, and Nelly the intimate gossip, but this cannot possibly be represented in a diagram.

Similarly, the family tree, which seems so innocuous, individualizes characters who are supposed to be somewhat confused. If *Wuthering Heights* makes characters difficult to distinguish, then perhaps we should be asking why this is so rather than trying to sort them out in charts. "Cathy two," to take the most obvious example, is in many ways a repetition of her mother: she certainly keeps "Cathy one's" spirit alive at Wuthering Heights. In other ways too, we have seen that the second generation is a repetition or parody of the first: Hareton is a duplication of Heathcliff's brutishness, and Linton is a grotesque parody of Edgar's sensitivity and delicacy. Similarly, Heathcliff's revenge is a parody of his oppressors: he beats the Lintons at their own game by appropriating their women and their property.

If Sanger's family tree had included surnames, it would have better demonstrated the *significance* of the names to the novel, but it would have been almost impossible to represent visually. Heathcliff, for example, has only one name, which signifies his dispossession: he is placed on the Linton side of the tree, through marriage, but he is given the first name only of the dead Heathcliff Earnshaw, the older son. Although Heathcliff appropriates Wuthering Heights, the house, he can never *be* an Earnshaw. The names Linton and Heathcliff double-up as Christian and surnames. There are two Hareton Earnshaws: one in the 1500s (the inscription over the door), and one in the 1800s. Wuthering Heights (the house) thus comes around full circle to be owned again by Hareton Earnshaw. Catherine's daughter Cathy is first Linton, then Heathcliff, then Earnshaw, which reverses her mother's scratched names on the window-pane, and signifies her feminine position as object of exchange along with the property. The names Earnshaw, Heathcliff, and Linton are similarly travelled full circle by the two Catherines: the same centripetal forces which represent the entitlement and enfranchisement of the men represent the oppressive constriction of the women. As you can see, the family tree masks the novel's probing of the complex interrelationships between names, property, and gender in the conferring of status.

David Musselwhite has shown that Brontë's juvenile poetry recasts the initials of characters in the Gondal saga over and over in different combinations. Musselwhite takes this as evidence of Brontë's fascination with the blurring of individual identity: it is difficult to see who is addressing whom.[3] *Wuthering Heights* expresses similarly unstable identities.

What business have we constructing explanatory diagrams for a book which begins and ends with a specter, in which even the distinction between being alive and being dead is uncertain and unclear? Catherine's ghost is perhaps the most important, and certainly the most pervasive, presence in the novel. The appearance of the ghost is that which prevents closure—that is, it inhibits any neat and tidy explanation of the novel; yet it is the ghost which is wholly ignored or repressed by genealogies, charts and diagrams. In order to listen to what Catherine's ghost is trying to tell us, to read the writing in the margin, we must avoid "the coercion of common sense" represented in the visual aids (*DM,* 154).

Notes and References

Chapter 1

1. Emily Brontë, *Wuthering Heights,* ed. David Daiches (1847; reprint, Harmondsworth: Penguin Books, 1985). All subsequent references to *Wuthering Heights* are cited in the text from this edition. Elizabeth Gaskell, *The Life of Charlotte Brontë,* ed. Alan Shelston (1924; Harmondsworth: Penguin Books, 1975); hereafter cited in text as *EG.*

2. Lyn Pykett, *Emily Brontë.* Women Writers Series. (Basingstoke: Macmillan, 1989), 1; hereafter cited in text as *LP.*

3. Juliet Barker, *The Brontës* (London: Weidenfeld and Nicolson, 1994), 271, 357; hereafter cited in text as *JB.*

4. See Juliet Barker (cited above), 271–72, 357–58, 453–54, and plate of one of the "Birthday Papers" between pp. 323–33.

5. M. Jeanne Peterson, "The Victorian Governess: Status Incongruence in Family and Society," in *Suffer and Be Still: Women in the Victorian Age,* ed. Martha Vicinus (Bloomington and London: Indiana Press, 1973), 3–19. Maggie Berg, *Jane Eyre: Portrait of a Life* (Boston: G. K. Hall & Co., 1987), 2.

6. Peter Stallybrass and Allon White, *The Politics and Poetics of Transgression* (London: Methuen, 1986), 2–3; hereafter cited in text as *S&W.*

7. Leonore Davidoff, "Gender and Class in Victorian England: The Diaries of Arthur J. Munby and Hannah Cullwick," *Feminist Studies* 5.1 (Spring 1979), 97; hereafter cited in text as *LD.*

8. For the home as an extension of the woman in Victorian thinking see John Ruskin, *Sesame and Lilies* (New York: John Wiley and Sons, 1890), 91. See also Davidoff cited above.

9. Quoted in Miriam Allott, ed., *The Brontës: The Critical Heritage* (London and Boston: Routledge & Kegan Paul, 1974), 222; hereafter cited in text as *CH.*

10. William Wordsworth, "Preface to the Second Edition of the Lyrical Ballads (1800)," in *Wordsworth: Selected Poems and Prefaces* ed. Jack Stillinger (Boston: Riverside Editions of Houghton Mifflin Co., 1965), 447.

11. Jacques Blondel, "Literary Influences in *Wuthering Heights*," in Miriam Allott, *Emily Brontë: Wuthering Heights*. Casebook Series. (Basingstoke & London: Macmillan Education, 1970), 234 ; hereafter cited in text as *MA*.

12. G. E. Harrison, *The Clue to the Brontës* (London: Methuen, 1948), 74.

13. Katherine M. Sorensen, "From Religious Ecstasy to Romantic Fulfillment: John Wesley's *Journal* and the Death of Heathcliff in *Wuthering Heights*," *The Victorian Newsletter* 82 (Fall 1992), 1–5.

14. Graham Holderness, *Wuthering Heights*. Open Guides to Literature Series. (Milton Keynes & Philadelphia: Open University Press, 1985), 20–21.

15. Robin Gilmour, "Scott and the Victorian Novel: The Case of 'Wuthering Heights,'" in J. H. Alexander and David Hewitt eds., *Scott and His Influence* (Aberdeen: Association for Scottish Literary Studies, 1983). See also Jacques Blondel, cited above.

16. David Wilson, "Emily Brontë: First of the Moderns," *Modern Quarterly Miscellany* 1 (1947), 96; hereafter cited in text as *DW*.

17. Terry Eagleton, *Heathcliff and the Great Hunger: Studies in Irish Culture* (London: Verso, 1995), 3.

18. Christopher Heywood, "Yorkshire Slavery in *Wuthering Heights*," *The Review of English Studies*, n.s. 38.150 (1987), 184–98; hereafter cited in text as *YS*. "A Yorkshire Background for *Wuthering Heights*," *The Modern Language Review* 88.4 (October 1993), 817–30; hereafter cited in text as *YB*.

19. Arnold Kettle, *An Introduction to the English Novel Volume 1* (1951; London: Hutchinson & Co., 1977), 140; hereafter cited in text as *AK*.

20. See Lisa Surridge, "Dogs' Bodies, Women's Bodies: Wives as Pets in Mid-Nineteenth-Century Narratives of Domestic Violence," *Victorian Review* 20.1 (Summer 1994), 1–33; hereafter cited in text as *LS*.

21. For the influence of the ballad, see Sheila Smith, "'At Once Strong and Eerie': The Supernatural in *Wuthering Heights* and its Debt to the Traditional Ballad," *The Review of English Studies* N.S.43.172 (1992), 498–517.

22. Vereen Bell, "*Wuthering Heights* as Epos," *College English* 25 (December 1963), 199–208.

Notes and References

Chapter 2

1. J. Hillis Miller, "Wuthering Heights: Repetition and the Uncanny," in his *Fiction and Repetition: Seven English Novels* (Cambridge, Mass.: Harvard University Press, 1982), 52; hereafter cited in text as *HM*.

2. Peter Miles, *Wuthering Heights*. The Critics Debate Series. (Basingstoke: Macmillan Education Ltd., 1990), 11; hereafter cited in text as *PM*.

3. To avoid confusion, this work will use "Catherine" for the mother and "Cathy" for the daughter throughout.

4. For an account of women readers' reactions see Sara Mills, Lynne Pearce, Sue Spaull, and Elaine Millard, eds., *Feminist Readings/Feminists Reading* (Charlottesville: University of Virginia Press, 1989), 76; hereafter cited in text as *F/R*.

5. David Musselwhite, "*Wuthering Heights:* The Unacceptable Text," in *Literature, Society, and the Sociology of Literature,* ed. Francis Barker (Colchester, Essex: Essex University Press, 1977), 154–60; hereafter cited in text as *DM*.

Chapter 3

1. Melvin Watson, "*Wuthering Heights* and the Critics," *Nineteenth Century Fiction* 3 (March 1949), 246; hereafter cited in text as *MW*.

2. A. C. Swinburne, "Emily Brontë," in *Miscellanies* (London: Chatto & Windus, 1886), 269; hereafter cited in text as *AS*.

3. C. P. Sanger, *The Structure of Wuthering Heights* (London: Hogarth Press, 1926); hereafter cited in text as *CS*.

4. David Cecil, "Emily Brontë and Wuthering Heights," in *Early Victorian Novelists: Essays in Revaluation* (1934; Harmondsworth: Pelican Books, 1948), 128; hereafter cited in text as *DC*.

5. Dorothy Van Ghent, "On *Wuthering Heights,*" in *The English Novel: Form and Function* (New York: Holt, Rinehart, and Winston, 1953), 157; hereafter cited in text as *VG*.

6. Eric Solomon, "The Incest Theme in *Wuthering Heights,*" *Nineteenth Century Fiction* 14 (June 1959), 80. Solomon points out that not only are Cathy and Heathcliff brother and sister, but also that "Heathcliff marries his lost love's sister-in-law, his wife's son marries her brother's daughter, Cathy's daughter marries *her* brother's son."

7. Thomas Moser, "What Is the Matter with Emily Jane?: Conflicting Impulses in *Wuthering Heights,*" *Nineteenth Century Fiction* 17.1 (June 1962), 1–19; hereafter cited in text as *TM*.

8. Elisabeth Th. M. Van de Laar, *The Inner Structure of Wuthering Heights: A Study of an Imaginative Field* (The Hague & Paris: Mouton, 1969), 12; hereafter cited in text as *VL*.

9. James Kavanagh, *Emily Brontë*. Rereading Literature Series. (Oxford: Basil Blackwell Ltd., 1985); hereafter cited in text as *JK*.

10. Terry Eagleton, *Myths of Power: A Marxist Study of the Brontës* (London: Macmillan, 1975), 100; hereafter cited in text as *TE*.

11. See Joanna Russ, *How To Suppress Women's Writing* (Austin: University of Texas Press, 1983), 21–22.

12. Inga-Stina Ewbank, *Their Proper Sphere: A Study of the Brontë Sisters as Early Victorian Female Novelists* (London: Edward Arnold, 1966), 87; hereafter cited in text as *IE*.

13. Sandra Gilbert and Susan Gubar, *The Madwoman in the Attic: The Woman Writer and the Nineteenth-Century Literary Imagination* (New Haven: Yale University Press, 1978); hereafter cited in text as *G&G*.

14. John Allen Stevenson, "Heathcliff is Me: *Wuthering Heights* and the Question of Likeness," *Nineteenth Century Literature* 43.1 (June 1988), 72; hereafter cited in text as *JS*.

15. Leo Bersani, *A Future For Astyanax: Character and Desire in Literature* (London: Marion Boyars, 1978), 198; hereafter cited in text as *LB*.

16. J. Hillis Miller, *The Disappearance of God* (Cambridge, Mass.: Harvard University Press, 1964), 172.

17. John Matthews, "Framing in Wuthering Heights," *Texas Studies in Literature and Language* 27.1 (Spring 1985), 29; hereafter cited in text as *JM*.

18. Linda Peterson, ed., *Emily Brontë: Wuthering Heights*. Case Studies in Contemporary Criticism Series. (Boston: Bedford Books of St. Martin's Press, 1992); hereafter cited in text as *CS*.

19. Beth Newman, "'The Situation of the Looker-On': Gender, Narration, and Gaze in *Wuthering Heights*," *PMLA* 105 (1990), 1029–41; hereafter cited in text as *BN*.

Chapter 4

1. See, for example, Dorothy Van Ghent, Lord David Cecil, and Terry Eagleton, cited above.

2. Gaston Bachelard, *The Poetics of Space,* trans. Maria Jolas (New York: Orion Press, 1964), 96; hereafter cited in text as *GB*.

3. Claude Levi-Strauss, *The Elementary Structures of Kinship* (Boston: Beacon Press, 1969), 481; hereafter cited in text as *L-S*.

4. Luce Irigaray, *This Sex Which Is Not One*, trans. Catherine Porter (New York: Cornell University Press, 1985), chaps. 4 and 7; hereafter cited in text as *TS*.

5. Mary Douglas, *Purity and Danger* (New York: Praeger Publishers Inc., 1966), 121; hereafter cited in text as *MD*.

Chapter 5

1. U. C. Knoepflmacher, *Emily Brontë: Wuthering Heights*. Landmarks of World Literature Series. (Cambridge: Cambridge University Press, 1989), 10; hereafter cited in text as *UK*.

2. For pets as women in nineteenth-century fiction see Lisa Surridge (*LS*) cited above.

3. Nancy Armstrong, *Desire and Domestic Fiction: A Political History of the Novel* (New York: Oxford University Press, 1987), 171; hereafter cited in text as *NA*.

4. Patricia Yaeger, "The Novel and Laughter: *Wuthering Heights*," in her *Honey-Mad Women: Emancipatory Strategies in Women's Writing* (New York: Columbia University Press, 1988), 179; hereafter cited in text as *PY*.

5. Carol Jacobs, "*Wuthering Heights:* At the Threshold of Interpretation," *Boundary 2: A Journal of Postmodern Literature and Culture* 7.3 (1979), 51; hereafter cited in text as *CJ*.

6. Sigmund Freud, "The Aetiology of Hysteria," (1896) in *The Freud Reader,* ed. Peter Gay (New York & London: W. W. Norton & Co., 1989), 97–98; hereafter cited in text as *SF*.

7. D. G. Rossetti, "The Orchard Pit," *Gabriel Charles Dante Rossetti: The Works,* ed. W. M. Rossetti (London: Ellis, 1911), 607–9.

8. See James Kavanagh, cited above (*JK,* 21–25), for the latest interpretation of the sexual nature of this scene.

9. Luce Irigaray, *Speculum of the Other Woman,* trans. Gillian C. Gill (New York: Cornell University Press, 1985), 50; hereafter cited in text as *SW*.

10. Barker Benfield, *The Horrors of the Half-Known Life: Male Attitudes Toward Women and Sexuality in Nineteenth-Century America* (New York: Harper & Row, 1976), 169; hereafter cited in text as *BB*.

11. F. R. Leavis, *The Great Tradition* (1948; Harmondsworth: Peregrine Books, 1962), 38; hereafter cited in text as *FL*.

12. Roland Barthes, *S/Z,* trans. Richard Miller (New York: Farrar, Strauss, and Giroux Inc., 1974), 4; see also "From Work to Text," in his *Image Music Text,* trans. Stephen Heath (London: Fontana Press, 1974), 162.

Chapter 6

1. Felicia Gordon, *A Preface to the Brontës* (London & New York: Longman, 1989), 200.

2. Toni Morrison, *Sula* (New York: Plume Books of New American Library, 1973), 58–63.

Chapter 7

1. Gayle Rubin, "The Traffic in Women: Notes on the 'Political Economy' of Sex," in *Toward an Anthropology of Women,* ed. Rayna Reiter (New York: Monthly Review Press, 1975), 157–210.

2. Eve Kosofsky Sedgwick, *Between Men: English Literature and Male Homosocial Desire* (New York: Columbia University Press, 1985), 2; hereafter cited in text as *ES.*

3. René Girard, *Deceit, Desire, and the Novel: Self and Other in Literary Structure.* trans. Yvonne Freccero (Baltimore: Johns Hopkins University Press, 1965), 7; hereafter cited in text as *RG.*

4. Lin Haire-Sargent, *H: The Story of Heathcliff's Journey Back to Wuthering Heights* (New York: Pocket Books, Simon & Schuster Inc., 1992), 107; hereafter cited in text as *H-S.*

5. N. M. Jacobs, "Gender and Layered Narrative in *Wuthering Heights* and *The Tenant of Wildfell Hall,*" *Journal of Narrative Technique* 16.3 (Fall 1986), 214.

6. Elizabeth Bronfen, *Over Her Dead Body: death, femininity and the aesthetic* (New York: Routledge, 1992), 225; hereafter cited in text as *EB.*

7. Juliet McMaster, "The Courtship and Honeymoon of Mr. and Mrs. Linton Heathcliff: Emily Brontë's Sexual Imagery," *Victorian Review* 1.18 (Summer 1992), 1–12.

8. See, for example, *F/R,* 76; *PY,* 203 (cited above).

9. A survey of women readers revealed that "Many women remarked on how attractive they found the prospect of a man loving them with such intensity" as Heathcliff loves Catherine (*F/R,* 76).

10. Jane Gallop, *The Daughter's Seduction* (Ithaca, New York: Cornell University Press, 1982), 37–38. I am grateful to Dana Medoro for pointing out to me that Heathcliff is "a prick."

Chapter 8

1. Wendy Craik, "The Brontës," in *The Victorians,* ed. Arthur Pollard (London: Barrie and Jenkins, 1970), 159.

2. For a good introduction to Jacques Lacan (who is notoriously difficult), see Judith Butler, *Subjects of Desire: Hegelian Reflections in Twentieth-Century France* (New York: Columbia University Press, 1987), 186–204.

3. See the painting of Charcot and a patient, "A Clinical Lecture at the Saltpêtrière," by André Brouillet, reproduced in Diane Hunter, "Hysteria, Psychoanalysis and Feminism: The Case of Anna O," in *The (M)other Tongue,* ed. Shirley Nelson Garner, Claire Kahane, and Madelon Spregnether (Ithaca & London: Cornell University Press, 1985), 108.

4.   It seems that even the critical tradition has met Catherine's hysteria with "belittling interpretations," since it has been generally ignored. A notable exception is Stevie Davies who, in *Emily Brontë: The Artist as Free Woman* (Manchester: Carcanet Press, 1983) sees this passage as symbolizing rebirth.

5.   See William Shakespeare, *Hamlet,* Act 5, sc. 5, lines 172ff.

Chapter 9

1.   Thomas Moser (*TM*) cited above, argues that "Emily Brontë loses control of the second half of her novel," and then asks how any critic "can take seriously the affair between Cathy and Hareton" (*TM,* 13, 15).

Chapter 10

1.   Alice Walker, *In Search of Our Mothers' Gardens* (San Diego: Harcourt Brace Jovanovich, 1983), 240, 241.

2.   See also Hélène Cixous, "The Laugh of the Medusa: Viewpoint," in *Signs: Journal of Women in Culture and Society* 1.4 (Summer 1976), 875–92.

Chapter 11

1.   Q. D. Leavis, "A Fresh Approach To *Wuthering Heights,*" in her *Lectures In America* (London: Chatto & Windus, 1969), 113.

2.   U. C. Knoepflmacher, *Emily Brontë: Wuthering Heights.* Landmarks of World Literature Series. (Cambridge: Cambridge University Press, 1989), 43, ix, xvii, 97, 54; hereafter cited as *UK.*

3.   David Musselwhite, *Partings Welded Together: Politics and Desire in the Nineteeth-Century English Novel* (London & New York: Methuen, 1987), 83–85.

Selected Bibliography

Primary Sources

Individual Works

Ellis Bell [pseud.] *Wuthering Heights: A Novel*. 3 vols. (vol 3: Acton Bell, *Agnes Grey*) London: Thomas Cautley Newby, Publisher, 1847.

Wuthering Heights. Edited by David Daiches. Harmondsworth: Penguin Books, 1985.

The Poems of Emily Brontë. Edited by Barbara Lloyd-Evans. London: B. T. Batsford Ltd., 1992.

Poems: by Currer, Ellis and Acton Bell. London: Aylott and Jones, 1846.

Juvenilia

Five Essays Written in French by Emily Jane Brontë. Translated by Lorine White Nagel. Introduction and notes by Fannie E. Ratchford. Austin: University of Texas Press, 1948.

Gondal's Queen: A Novel in Verse. Edited by Fannie E. Ratchford. Austin: University of Austin Press, 1955.

Collected Editions

The Shakespeare Head Brontë. Edited by Thomas James Wise and John Alexander Symington. 19 vols. Oxford: Shakespeare Head Press, 1931–38. Includes novels, life and letters, poems, miscellaneous, and unpublished writings.

Selected Bibliography

Letters

Shorter, Clement, ed. *The Brontës: Life and Letters.* 2 vols. London: Hodder & Stoughton, 1908; New York: Haskell House (1908) 1969.

Wise, Thomas James, and John Alexander Symington, eds. *The Brontës: Their Lives, Friendships and Correspondence.* 4 vols. Oxford: Shakespeare Head Press, 1932. Reprint (4 vols. in 2) Oxford: Basil Blackwell, 1980.

Secondary Sources

Bibliographies

Barclay, Janet M. *Emily Brontë Criticism 1900–1982: An Annotated Checklist.* Westport, Connecticut & London: Meckler Publishing, 1984.

Miles, Peter. *Wuthering Heights.* The Critics Debate Series. London: Macmillan, 1990. An excellent thematic delineation of various critical approaches to *Wuthering Heights,* with the author's own appraisal of the novel.

Watson, Melvin. "Wuthering Heights and the Critics." *Nineteenth Century Fiction* 3 (March 1949): 243–63.

Biographies

Barker, Juliet. *The Brontës.* London: Weidenfeld and Nicolson, 1994.

Davies, Stevie. *Emily Brontë: The Artist as a Free Woman.* Manchester: Carcanet Press, 1983.

Frank, Katherine. *Chainless Soul: A Life of Emily Brontë.* Boston: Houghton Mifflin, 1990. A highly readable biography which sees Emily Brontë as suffering from anorexia nervosa.

Gérin, Winifred. *Emily Brontë: A Biography.* Oxford: Oxford University Press, 1972.

Books

Eagleton, Terry. *Myths of Power: A Marxist Study of the Brontës.* London: The Macmillan Press Ltd., 1975. Sees the Brontë novels as expressions of the sisters' painfully ambiguous position in the social structure at the time. Claims that the "natural" love of Catherine and Heathcliff is outside of Victorian social convention.

Ewbank, Inga-Stina. *Their Proper Sphere: A Study of the Brontë Sisters as Early-Victorian Female Novelists.* London: Edward Arnold Ltd., 1966. An early feminist (and humanist) account. It has a very useful first chapter which places the Brontës in the context of women writers of the 1840s.

Holderness, Graham. *Wuthering Heights.* Open Guides to Literature Series. Milton Keynes and Philadelphia: Open University Press, 1985. A thought-provoking discussion of selected passages from the novel which avoids imposing definitive answers to key issues raised by the text.

Kavanagh, James. *Emily Brontë.* Rereading Literature Series. Oxford: Basil Blackwell, 1985. A psychoanalytic and Marxist interpretation of the "textual ideology" of *Wuthering Heights.* A difficult but stimulating reading of the novel.

Peterson, Linda H. *Emily Brontë: Wuthering Heights.* Case Studies in Contemporary Criticism Series. Boston: Bedford Books of St. Martin's Press, 1992. Basingstoke: Macmillan Press, 1992. This is an edition of the text with biographical, historical, and critical information, and five essays exhibiting different critical approaches. What makes this book noteworthy is the inclusion of sections explaining deconstruction, cultural criticism, and other approaches, with suggestions for further reading in theory as well as criticism.

Pykett, Lyn. *Emily Brontë.* Women Writers Series. Basingstoke and London: Macmillan Education Ltd., 1989. A fascinating yet accessible feminist account of the poetry and the novel focusing on the construction of Emily Brontë, the question of gender and genre, and the women characters in *Wuthering Heights.*

Van de Laar, Elisabeth Th. M. *The Inner Structure of Wuthering Heights: A Study of an Imaginative Field.* The Hague: Mouton & Co. N. V., 1969. A fascinating comprehensive study of the imagery in *Wuthering Heights* of the elements, the weather, dreams, windows, books, animals, and others.

Chapters or Essays in Other Books

Bersani, Leo. "Desire and Metamorphosis." In *A Future for Astyanax: Character and Desire in Literature,* 189–229. Boston: Little, Brown and Co., 1976. An early poststructuralist approach. A stimulating argument that *Wuthering Heights* dramatizes "frenetic uncertainty about the very possibility of being," and that Brontë employs "genealogy as a pretext for depersonalisation." Also argues that the narrative structure of the novel "expels difference," because events return to a point of origin.

Cecil, David. "Emily Brontë and Wuthering Heights." in *Early Victorian Novelists: Essays in Revaluation.* London: Constable & Co., 1934. Harmondsworth: Pelican Books, 1948, 115–51. Extremely influential study of the novel. Brontë was "a mystic" who beheld a "transcendental reality," and who saw human beings only in relation "to the cosmic scheme." *Wuthering Heights* dramatizes the conviction that the cosmos is animated by a conflict between the "principle of storm" and "the principle of calm."

Selected Bibliography

Gilbert, Sandra M., and Susan Gubar. "Looking Oppositely: Emily Brontë's Bible of Hell." In *The Madwoman in the Attic: The Woman Writer and the Nineteenth Century Literary Imagination.* New Haven: Yale University Press, 1979, 248–308. Argues that in *Wuthering Heights* Brontë, a "rebellious child" of Milton, reverses the myth of *Paradise Lost.* Like Blake, Brontë thought in polarities. Argues also that Heathcliff is "female" on an "associative level."

Kettle, Arnold. "Emily Brontë: Wuthering Heights." In *An Introduction to the English Novel,* 2 vols. I:139–53. London: Hillary House, 1951. An early Marxist reading which can be seen as a direct response to David Cecil (above). Argues that Catherine and Heathcliff invert the "common standards of bourgeois morality," and that Heathcliff retains our sympathy because he uses the weapons of his oppressors against them, but comes to recognize the "hollowness of his victory."

Miller, J. Hillis. "Wuthering Heights: Repetition and the Uncanny." In *Fiction and Repetition: Seven English Novels,* 41–72. Cambridge, Massachusetts: Harvard University Press, 1982. A deconstructive reading which analyzes the "uncanny" effect of infinite repetition in *Wuthering Heights.* Makes the provocative argument that all the different critical accounts of the novel mistakenly pursue "some origin, end, or underlying ground" which "would explain all the enigmatic incongruities of what is visible." Concludes that Charlotte Brontë's Preface seems muddled because it repeats the "alogic" of Emily Brontë's text.

Musselwhite, David. "Wuthering Heights: the Unacceptable Text." In *Literature, Society and the Sociology of Literature,* edited by Francis Barker, 154–60. Essex: University of Essex Press, 1977. One of my two favorite essays, which argues that *Wuthering Heights* demonstrates how literature is used "as an instrument of ideology." Draws attention to the existence of an "unacceptable" text in *Wuthering Heights.*

Articles

McMaster, Juliet. "The Courtship and Honeymoon of Mr. and Mrs. Linton Heathcliff: Emily Brontë's Sexual Imagery." *Victorian Review* 1. 18 (Summer 1992): 1–12. One of the very few essays on *Wuthering Heights* to deal with the abuse of the women and the sexual nature of the violence; an excellent reading of Heathcliff's battering of Cathy as a symbolic consummation of her marriage to Linton.

Moser, Thomas. "What Is the Matter With Emily Jane? Conflicting Impulses in *Wuthering Heights.*" *Nineteenth Century Fiction* 17.1 (June 1962): 1–19. An infuriatingly condescending but otherwise provocative argument that *Wuthering Heights* is all about sex. Heathcliff embodies the id: he is an amoral consuming sexual force. Betrays Moser's intense attraction to Heathcliff.

Newman, Beth. " 'The Situation of the Looker-On': Gender, Narration, and Gaze in *Wuthering Heights.*" *Publications of the Modern Language Association* 105 (1990): 1029–41. My favorite essay on *Wuthering Heights.* Analyzes "the sexual politics of looking" in *Wuthering Heights,* in which the female gaze (like Medusa's) threatens the male spectator with castration. Also links the "specular economy" to the process of novelistic narrative.

Wilson, David. "Emily Brontë: First of the Moderns." *Modern Quarterly Miscellany* 1 (1947): 94–115. Pioneering of Marxist, or cultural materialist, readings of the novel. The focus is on Brontë herself in her socio-historical context. Brontë is shown, through her writings, to have "close sympathy . . . with the common people of her time and place."

Index

animal imagery. *See* imagery
Armstrong, Nancy, 19

Bachelard, Gaston, 25–26
Barker, Juliet, 3
Barthes, Roland, 40
Bell, Ellis (pseudonym). *See* Brontë,
    Emily
Bell, Vereen, 7
Bersani, Leo, 18, 89, 99
Bewick, Thomas, 85
Blackwood's Magazine, 5
Branwell, Elizabeth (aunt of Emily
    Brontë), 5
Bronfen, Elizabeth, 63, 66
Brontë, Anne (sister of Emily
    Brontë), 3, 6
Brontë, Charlotte (sister of Emily
    Brontë): *Jane Eyre,* 6; relation-
    ship with Emily Brontë, 3;
    writings compared to Emily
    Brontë's, 4; *Wuthering*

Heights, preface of, 3, 11–15,
    16, 19, 20, 35, 57
Brontë, Emily: bird imagery used by,
    85; challenge to phallocen-
    trism of, 27; class status of, 4;
    domestic chores of, 5; poetry
    of, 3, 4, 14, 117; pseudonym
    of, 3, 14; reclusiveness of,
    3–4, 13; relationship with
    Charlotte Brontë, 3; religious
    views of, 45; reviewers and,
    89, 112, 115; teaching career
    of, 4; writings compared to
    Catherine's, 4
Byron, George Gordon, 5

Catherine: death of, 25, 53–54, 57,
    65, 66, 71, 77, 83–88, 92,
    114; diary of, 4, 24, 26–27,
    32–33, 36–43, 46, 49, 50,
    75–76, 81, 84, 86, 88, 102,
    104, 107, 108, 114; Edgar

Index

116; racial, 6, 80; satiric, 39;
spatial, 23–26, 27, 40, 43, 90
In Search of Our Mothers' Gardens
(Alice Walker), 107–8
*Inner Structure of Wuthering Heights,
The* (Elizabeth Van de Laar),
16
Irigaray, Luce: on female hysteria,
83; on female sexuality,
34–35, 52, 64, 72; on patriarchy, 27, 38–39, 62, 65,
75–76, 77, 86; on subversion,
109, 113; on Western dis-
course, 47
Isabella: death of, 67; Edgar and, 63;
Heathcliff and, 26, 49, 54–59,
62–66, 70, 82, 92, 95, 100,
105, 110, 115; inheritance of,
91; Nelly and, 50, 51, 110, 115

Jacobs, Carol, 32, 33, 34
Jacobs, Naomi, 63
Jane Eyre (Charlotte Brontë), 6
Joseph: Catherine and, 38–40,
44–45; Cathy and, 37, 39,
46–47, 103–5, 107–9; characterization of, 24; ghosts and,
114; Hareton and, 46, 47,
103, 108; Heathcliff and, 39,
45, 46, 58, 92, 108; Hindley
and, 45; Linton and, 94, 95;
Lockwood's dreams and, 33,
48; phallocentric approach to
texts of, 26; traditional values
of, 5, 44–51, 54, 75, 108

Kavanagh, James: critical approach
of, 16, 19; on Heathcliff,
65–66, 91; on Nelly as narrator, 48
Kettle, Arnold, 55, 91
Knoepflmacher, U. C., 114–16

Lacan, Jacques, 81

laughter, 109–10
Leavis, F. R., 40
Levi-Strauss, Claude, 26, 56
Life of Charlotte Brontë (Elizabeth
Gaskell), 3
Linton (Heathcliff's son): Cathy and,
56, 64, 90–91, 93, 97–99,
100–104; Edgar and, 93–94,
98, 116; Hareton and, 94–95;
Heathcliff and, 90–95, 97;
Joseph and, 94, 95; Nelly and,
93–95
Linton, Catherine. *See* Catherine
Linton, Edgar. *See* Edgar
Linton, Isabella. *See* Isabella
Lockwood: animal imagery and, 59;
aperture imagery and, 29;
Catherine's diary and, 32–33,
36–43, 46, 74, 84; Cathy and,
30, 31, 37, 46, 78, 90, 101,
105, 112; Edgar and, 61;
entrance to Wuthering Heights
of, 28–32, 58; Hareton and,
30; Heathcliff and, 28–29, 30,
35, 36, 57, 58, 88; Nelly and,
32, 52, 112, 115; nightmares
of, 32–37, 39, 41, 46, 48, 60,
98; phallocentric approach to
texts of, 26, 57, 71, 75; spatial
characterization of, 24, 25; as
surrogate reader, 28, 32, 40,
75, 114
London Labour and the London Poor
(Henry Mayhew), 4

marriage, 56, 63
Marx, Karl, 6
Marxist criticism, 17
Mary Barton (Elizabeth Gaskell), 6
masturbation. *See* sexuality
Matthews, John, 19
Mayhew, Henry, 4
McMaster, Juliet, 64
Miles, Peter, 15, 18, 73, 87

Index

Mill on the Floss, The (George Eliot), 77

Miller, J. Hillis: on enigmatic character of *Wuthering Heights*, 9, 20, 111; poststructuralist critiques of, 18–19

Morrison, Toni, 54

Moser, Thomas: on Emily Brontë and sex, 16; on Cathy's feminization effect, 89, 98, 100, 104; on Heathcliff, 67; on *Wuthering Heights* conclusion, 112

Musselwhite, David: on Emily Brontë's poetry, 117; on Catherine's ghost, 10, 74, 114; on Lockwood's dreams, 34, 35; on Marxist criticism, 17

Nelly: Catherine and, 49–52, 77–81, 83–85, 87; Cathy and, 49, 50, 92, 99, 101–2, 106–7; Edgar and, 49, 50, 52, 68, 71; ghosts and, 114; Hareton and, 53, 54, 56, 95; Heathcliff and, 49–51, 58–61, 63–65, 93, 96, 98; Hindley and, 53, 54, 64; Isabella and, 50, 51, 110, 115; Joseph and, 45, 47, 53; Linton and, 93–95; Lockwood and, 32, 52, 112, 115; as narrator, 48, 115–16; nest imagery and, 54, 73; phallocentric approach to texts of, 26, 27, 52; spatial characterization of, 24–26; traditional values of, 39, 44, 48–54, 89

nest imagery. *See* imagery

Newman, Beth: critical perspective of, 20; on male fears of female sexuality, 31, 77–78, 103, 107

Oliver Twist (Charles Dickens), 6

oral traditions, 7

Orchard Pit, The (D.G. Rossetti), 33

Othello (William Shakespeare), 45

patriarchy: devaluation of women under, 6, 7, 10, 53, 54, 56, 62, 65, 76, 77, 86, 99, 104, 117; Luce Irigaray on, 27, 38–39, 62, 65, 75–76, 77, 86; Claude Levi-Strauss on, 26, 56; masculinity and, 62; Nelly as upholder of, 49–52, 54; phallocentric approach to texts under, 75; violence and, 65

poststructuralist criticism, 18–19

psychoanalytic criticism, 16, 19, 20

Pykett, Lyn, 3, 18, 52

religion: critical perspective on, 18–19; fanaticism and, 5, 45; Joseph's use of, 45–48, 54; Nelly's use of, 50–52, 54

romanticism, 15, 16, 19

Rossetti, D.G., 33

Rubin, Gayle, 56

Sanger, C.P., 15, 115, 116

satire, 39, 45

Scott, Sir Walter, 5

Sedgwick, Eve, 56, 60–61

sexuality: castration fears and, 37, 46–48, 60, 78; defiant women and, 31, 47, 77–78, 101–3, 107–9, 113; Luce Irigaray on, 34–35, 52; masturbation and, 35–36, 37, 38, 105; phallocentric approach to texts and, 75; pregnancy deaths and, 87; rites of passage in, 60, 92, 102; texts and, 57, 90, 101, 107, 113; Victorian ideology on, 35–36, 37; violence and, 10, 53, 54, 64, 73

Shakespeare, William, 45

Shuttelworth, James, 29
spatial analysis: characterization through, 23–26, 27, 40, 90; masculinity and, 43; violence toward women and, 58, 72; visual aids and, 115
Stallybrass, Peter, 27, 30, 31
Stevenson, John Allen, 18, 82
Sula (Toni Morrison), 54
Surridge, Lisa, 30
Swinburne, Algernon Charles, 15

Tenant of Wildfell Hall, The (Anne Brontë), 6
texts: Luce Irigaray on, 38–39, 65; phallocentric approach to, 26, 27, 32–34, 39, 45–46, 52, 71, 75; sexuality and, 57, 90, 101, 107, 113; spatial metaphors and, 43; women as, 26–27, 57, 66, 71, 74–75, 90, 97, 101, 104–7, 113

Van de Laar, Elizabeth: on Edgar, 68; on Heathcliff, 59, 64, 67–68, 101; on imagery, 16, 23, 29, 58; on Joseph, 44; on Nelly, 48, 51
Van Ghent, Dorothy, 15, 16
Victorian ideology: middle-class formation and, 4–5, 29; sexuality and, 35–36, 37; subversion of, 4, 102, 110; women's status under, 5, 18, 25, 29, 30, 33, 94, 102, 110
violence: critics' reaction to, 10, 12, 15; Hareton and, 44, 90, 100, 103, 106; Heathcliff and, 26, 55, 57–59, 62–66, 68–69, 90, 91–95, 100, 103–4, 106, 110; Lockwood and, 30; patriarchy and, 10, 65; sexuality and, 10, 53, 54, 64, 73; toward

women, 10, 26, 44, 55, 57–58, 62–67, 72, 78, 93, 100, 103–4

Walker, Alice, 107–8
Watson, Melvin, 15
Wesley, John, 5
White, Allon, 27, 30, 31
Wilson, David, 16–17
women: animal representations of, 30, 31–32, 58–59, 63, 65, 70, 100; Sigmund Freud and, 33; patriarchical oppression of, 6, 7, 10, 53, 54, 56, 62, 65, 76, 77, 86, 99, 104, 117; sexual defiance by, 31, 47, 77–78, 101–3, 107–9, 113; as texts, 26–27, 57, 66, 71, 74–75, 90, 97, 101, 104–7, 113; Victorian ideology on, 5, 18, 25, 29, 30, 33, 94, 102, 110; violence toward, 10, 26, 44, 55, 57–58, 62–67, 72, 78, 93, 100, 103–4
Wordsworth, William, 5
Wuthering Heights (Emily Brontë): Charlotte Brontë's preface for, 3, 11–15, 16, 19, 20, 35, 57; Gothic elements in, 5–6, 7, 8; literary influences on, 5, 8; movie versions of, 9, 89, 90, 112; narrative structure of, 8–9, 28, 48, 115–16; oral traditions and, 7; reviews of, 5, 8, 9, 11–20, 27, 28, 37, 74, 84–85, 89, 110, 111–12, 114; significance of names in, 116–17; visual aids for, 9, 20, 114–17

Yaeger, Patricia, 30, 74, 110

Zillah, 94, 104, 107

The Author

Maggie Berg is Associate Professor at Queen's University in Ontario, where she teaches Victorian literature and literary theory, especially feminist theory. She has published articles and chapters on the Pre-Raphaelites and on the French feminist Luce Irigaray. She is author of the *Jane Eyre* volume in Twayne's series of Masterwork Studies. She is co-editing a collection of essays on domestic violence in Victorian literature, and is currently writing on Anne Brontë.